The Kunshan Way

FOREIGN LANGUAGES PRESS

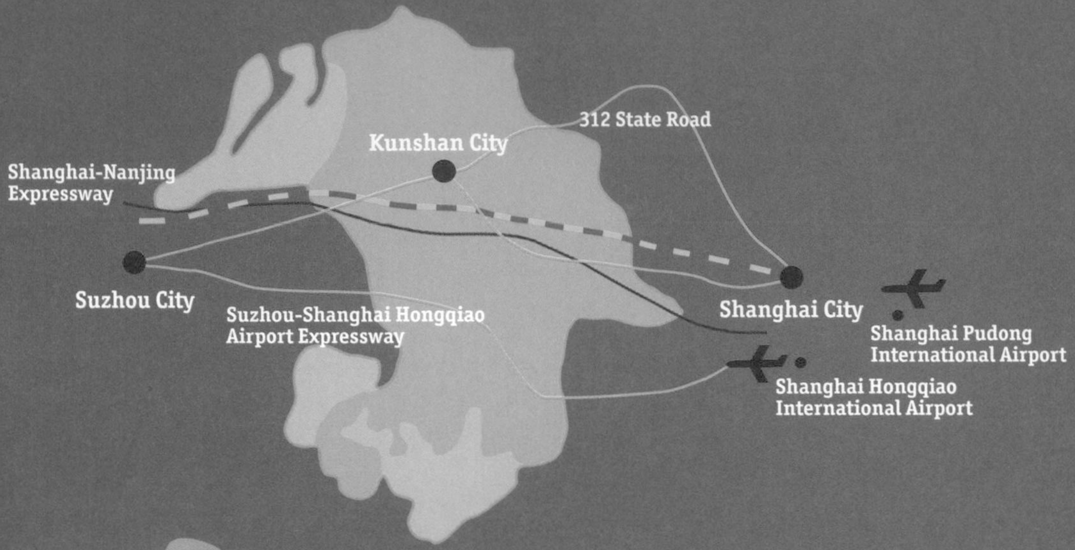

Shanghai-Nanjing
Expressway

Kunshan City

312 State Road

Suzhou City

Suzhou-Shanghai Hongqiao
Airport Expressway

Shanghai City

Shanghai Pudong
International Airport

Shanghai Hongqiao
International Airport

Bacheng Township

Zhoushi Township

Yushan Township

Kunshan City
(County-level)

Shanghai City
(Municipality)

Lujia Township

Suzhou City
(Prefecture-level)

Zhangpu Township

Huaqiao Township

Qiandeng Township

Jinxi Township

Dianshan Lake Township

Zhouzhuang Township

Geographical Zoning Map

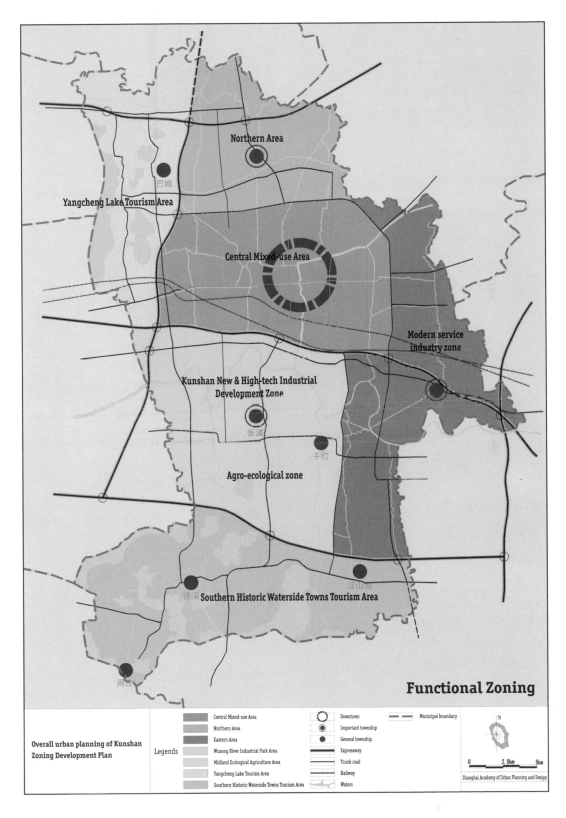

Northern Area

巴城

Yangcheng Lake Tourism Area

Central Mixed-use Area

昆山市区域

Modern service industry zone

Kunshan New & High-tech Industrial Development Zone

张浦

千灯

Agro-ecological zone

锦溪

淀山湖

Southern Historic Waterside Towns Tourism Area

周庄

Functional Zoning

Overall urban planning of Kunshan Zoning Development Plan

Legends

	Central Mixed-use Area
	Northern Area
	Eastern Area
	Wusong River Industrial Park Area
	Midland Ecological Agriculture Area
	Yangcheng Lake Tourism Area
	Southern Historic Waterside Towns Tourism Area

	Downtown
	Important township
	General township
	Expressway
	Trunk road
	Railway
	Waters

Municipal boundary

N

0   2.5km   5km

Shanghai Academy of Urban Planning and Design

Cities of China

The China International Publishing Group's Foreign Languages Press is currently publishing the "Cities of China" series. I believe this is very timely move, and one of great significance.

The Ancient Greek philosopher Aristotle once said, "Men come together in cities in order to live; they remain together in order to enjoy life."

In 1800, only two percent of the world's population lived in cities. By 2007, this rate had soared to over 50 percent. The UN predicts that by 2010 urban dwellers will make up 55 percent of the world's total population. Today, the pace and scale of urbanization, which is unprecedented in the history of humanity, indicates that the world is entering a new era.

The steady rise of a group of developing countries represents one of the most striking trends in international relations of this century. The population of these countries adds up to over half of the world's total population. The level of change and the number of countries involved are also unprecedented in human history. All the countries concerned share one common feature, that is, they are going through a simultaneous process of industrialization and urbanization. In the context of the rapid and extensive urbanization, due attention must be paid to the challenges the cities face.

In this regard, the theme "Better City, Better Life" of the 2010 World Expo Shanghai, China, responds to the tide of human development. It is the first time in the World Expo history that the city becomes the theme, as confirmed by the support from the Bureau of International Exhibitions (BIE) members.

The "Cities of China" series is characterized by a foreign perspective on China's cities. As the world's oldest civilization with an uninterrupted history going back thousands of years, China boasts a profound urban culture which constitutes an important component of its civilization. The world's first city with a population of half a million was Linzi in China, and the world's first city with a one million population, Chang'an (today's Xi'an), was also in China. Today, fast-developing cities of all sizes are scattered throughout the country. Among them, metropolises like Beijing and Shanghai are well-known throughout the world while smaller ones, though less known, have their own charms. They are the focus of the "Cities of China" series. New and dynamic cities like Nanjing, Kunshan, Nantong and Wuxi covered by this series will help the readers know better China's urbanization and development.

The books in this series are written by foreign writers familiar with an English-speaking readership. They show the important aspects of Chinese cities and their cultures.

The past 100 years have witnessed many twists and turns in China's revolution and rebuilding. There was a period in which we severely criticized and even negated our own culture. Now, however, with China's rise, our people are becoming ever more appreciative of their own culture and are trying to rediscover it. The "Cities of China" series is designed to assist with this process. People from other countries have a perspective that is quite different from our own. They are more likely to notice the things that we take for granted and overlook. As a Chinese idiom says, "Advice from others may help one overcome one's shortcomings." An outsider's view of China's cities can give us a broader picture of our own urban culture.

Western culture has made great contributions to the world. Without it, we would not have been in a position to enjoy our material wealth and our rapidly-developing science and technology. The whole world has something to learn from Western culture. But, we also have to realize that Western culture, like any other culture, has its own weaknesses. While it has certainly driven human civilization forward, it has brought with it many problems. Over the past few centuries, the world has been dominated by Western culture, and the Eastern contributions have been overlooked. In the 21st century, it is time once again for Eastern culture to make its presence felt. The "Cities of China" series can help the world to better understand and learn from the East, and thereby find solutions to the problems created by and faced by all our cities.

The Shanghai World Expo in China is a great event for human civilization. The publishing of this series will make a significant contribution to the World Expo movement. I wish it great success!

Wu Jianmin
Honorary President of the Bureau of International Exhibitions
April 2010, Beijing

Dedication

This book is dedicated to the officials you rarely hear about, those who actually devote their lives to serving the people.

Preface

China ranks No. 1 in economic and per-capita income growth, holds the largest foreign exchange reserves, is the third largest economy in the world, yet I know of few people from outside the country who can name any of its provinces or more than three of its cities. How is it possible that we know so little about a country which figures so largely in the world today? While there are a number of reasons, one is the lack of reliable information about how its economy functions and the part provinces and cities play in it.

This book is the first in a series of economic tour guides which present the numbers in the context of the system and people which created them. Kunshan was chosen because it has accomplished more in its 20 years of existence than any other city like it in China. It is also significant because it is a city which, unknown to you, touches you and the people you know on a daily basis.

Actually, selecting Kunshan was a lot easier than figuring out how to express its success. After staying in Kunshan, observing the people and interviewing its government and business leaders, it was clear that there is more to Kunshan than numbers. In many respects, China is too vast to handle easily. It's hard to comprehend a country which has moved more people out of poverty in 30 years than the total population of the United States, but still has twice that number waiting in the wings. In the same way, it is hard to express how a rural township like Kunshan went in 20 years from providing the majority of grain in the Suzhou area to manufacturing the majority of laptops for the world. Everyone I talked to, in Kunshan, was quick to point to the proximity to Shanghai, inexpensive labor and low development costs. But, given these factors are shared with all of the communities that surround Shanghai and many other major cities in China, the question remained: why had Kunshan risen to the top?

Kunshan, like every city in the world, has a character that defines it as a place and a city. Can you imagine someone trying to define New York, London, Paris, without referencing the characteristics of the people? Add the fact that China is more diverse in terms of different languages, food, customs and climate than any Western developed nation. For those who think people in southern and northern Germany, France, or the US are different, at least they speak the same language.

In Kunshan, the locals speak a local language which is close to, but different from their immediate neighbor Shanghai. While most today speak Mandarin, some of the older generations do not. The differences extend beyond dialect to physical attributes, character and food, despite the fact that they share a common heritage and border.

The difference is, Kunshan is just one of 500 Chinese cities with more than 500,000 people, whereas the US has only 33 cities of comparable size. Kunshan is larger than Philadelphia, Phoenix, Atlanta, Algiers, Vienna, Hamburg and Perth, but unlike those cities it is a fifth-level city that few have heard of outside of China.

The task of trying to describe Kunshan is not easy. But, if you have the chance to walk around Kunshan, you will immediately get what I can not adequately describe, a town of bustling streets, where electric bikes share roads and sidewalks with cars and people, where unremarkable 80 and 90's buildings sit next to new architectural creations and centuries-old structures, where cabbies listen to the foreign exchange report and neighbors exchange gossip over tea ,just as they have for thousands of years, where modern factories sit across from ancient farm fields and hi-tech businesses and fishermen ply their trades side by side, one in their research facility on riverbank and the other on the river within their traditional boats. I hope when you read the interviews and commentary you will see the differences which are responsible for Kunshan and China's growth and understand that Kunshan is just one of many places you need to get to know if you want to do business in or with China.

For those of you who read this while the 2010 Shanghai World Expo is going on, I hope you will take the half hour train ride to Kunshan and see for yourself how change has come to China. "Better City, Better Life" is the theme of the Expo and if you want to understand and experience how one of China's leading cities is making this happen, it would be well worth the trip to Kunshan. Regardless of whether you're interested in doing business in Kunshan or just trying to discover the essence of China yesterday and today, there are few places that can give you so much of both. As it is, China sits at the crossroads of a new era where its influence will be as important to the world as the world's influence was to China for the last 30 years. The Kunshan Way is a sign post which can help you understand China past and future.

I would like to thank the following people:

Huang Youyi, Vice President and Editor-in-Chief of China International Publishing Group (CIPG), for his friendship, intelligence and support of projects which express the reality of China;

Foreign Languages Press' Li Zhenguo, Xie Chen, Nicole Ouyang, Wen Fang and all others who assisted in publishing this book;

Mr. Gao Zhanxiang, former Vice Minister of Culture, author, artist, dancer and photographer, who has shown me that how inextricably linked culture and economics are;

Ms. Gao Yan, for her insights and inspiration;

Yang Shikun whose tireless work has made the book possible;

Ms. Gao Lili and Ms. Hu Tao for their research on cultural and historical issues and support; and Mr. Zhao Yiyang for providing invaluable research on the structure and economics of Chinese cities;

Officials of Kunshan for their time, efforts and patience, including Mr. Xu Yulian, Mr. Jin Jianhong, Ms. Zhou Ming, Mr. Dai Xiaohua, Mr.Yang Xinfeng, Ms.Yang Qiong and Ms. Liu Li (Kunshan Bureau of Commerce) for their extraordinary efforts and hard work in arranging interviews and hospitality;

Mr. Li Pengju, our Kunshan-based photographer who provided many of the beautiful pictures you will see.

Contents

Chapter 1
China and the Kunshan Way

If you are interested in how China has risen so quickly, the Kunshan Way will show you part of the equation. But, to understand it, you will need to keep four things in mind: China operates on a different set of social and economic assumptions; China's government structure is a top-down hierarchy; the things you hear and read about China are often misleading; and the best way to understand China is to go to Kunshan. If you do, I can promise you it will be a pleasant and enlightening experience.

Lou River—Kunshan's "Mother River"

Different Assumptions

Put simply, it is about how the process is being driven. In the US, we believe that a prosperous and stable society can only be achieved through the "free market mechanism," in China they believe that a "harmonious and sustainable society" can only be achieved through centrally orchestrated planning and implementation. The issue is not whether you agree or disagree, it is just that you understand that there is a different set of assumptions.

Kuilei Lake—Kunshan's water reservoir

Top-down Hierarchy

While there are many different types of government structures in the West, few go as far as China in terms of a centrally planned and managed system. The system has two components—the Communist Party and the government—which often seem to be one in the same, but are functionally distinct. Both share a top-down structure where political policies and operational directives are made in Beijing and sent to the provinces and municipalities to be implemented.

Misconceptions

One of the other major barriers we face in trying to understand China is the popular misconceptions that dominate people's thinking and the media. The leading four are: the basic lack of knowledge about the country, its history, culture and structure of its government; the constant flow of "China business books" with their anecdotal tunnel vision focusing on how to make money in China; the never ending stream of articles, books and talking heads who see China's economic development as a "long-march" political strategy; and the unfortunate fact that the voices and experiences of those who have been shaping China's economic development, while vigorously debating and discussing the issues internally, have been largely silent when it comes to broadcasting their views to the rest of the world.

Ignorance

A few years ago, I was trying to set up a meeting between the governor of Wisconsin and Deng Pufang. I was talking to the person in charge of the International Department for the Wisconsin Department of Commerce. I kept emphasizing that in addition to being the chairman of the China Disabled Persons Federation, he was the son of Deng Xiaoping. After a number of exasperating minutes, she asked me, "Why do you keep mentioning this Deng Xiaoping person?" I asked her if she had heard of Mao Zedong. Answer: "Yes. Well Deng had a similar role after Mao." There was a bit of silence and then the conversation moved on. China was Wisconsin's fourth largest trading partner at the time.

Self-Interest: Cheap Labor and Globalization

Jack Perkowski was promoting his book *Managing the Dragon* to a club I am part of. He was what you would expect of an offensive lineman/investment banker-turned China business mogul. He gave a slightly varied version of the "white man's economic burden" where he generously took partial responsibility for bringing China into the global economy, as he was making a fortune. He was less responsive when I asked him, in essence, how the natives would fare in the future without their "great white chief." Let me be clear, he was an effective speaker and pleasant enough person, but the focus of his book, like so many others like it, reduced China to an economic cog in some global dash for cash. This type of self-righteous economic colonialism may be in vogue, but it is a flawed rationalization which has led to more tears than gold.

On the right:
Zhouzhuang, China's best-known ancient water town

The Game Theorists: "China Inc." and the "Beijing Consensus"

A number of Western politicians/intellectuals have developed and promoted various ideas, including "China Inc.: How the Rise of the Next Superpower Challenges America and the World" by Ted C. Fishman and the "Beijing Consensus" by Joshua Cooper Ramo. The cruxes of these views are that China's economic rise is part of a calculated economic/political agenda. Unfortunately, they ignore the more persuasive evidence, which suggests that China's development has been more of a "construct," a mixture of capitalism, communism, democracy and socialism, governed by pragmatism, rather than some covert world domination plan.

Chinese chess

The simple fact is, China is a large country with a low ratio of resources per person, which, despite its success, has 800 million people anxiously waiting for the Chinese dream to reach them. Unfortunately, simplified conspiracy theories resonate more with audiences than the more mundane realities of economic and social development.

This is not to say that China, as a nation, does not have defined political and economic goals and strategies. In the past, other than competing for resources, China has been more internally than externally focused. Today, that is changing rapidly, as China's economic success has generated social and political repercussions.

Previously, the developing world looked to the West for socioeconomic development models. Today, developing countries, while they desire the prosperity enjoyed by first-tier nations, look at places like China for models on how to get there. In this reality, viewing China through the lenses of our own assumptions and beliefs is not only useless but dangerous. Understanding what China is, how it operates and its goals is now a necessity.

The Silence of China

Although debated, discussed and written about extensively within China, few Chinese intellectuals or pundits have had success popularizing their views in other languages. Whether this is due to China's traditional inward-facing emphasis, cultural reticence or a lack of confidence is a matter for a different debate. What is clear is that China's silence has created a vacuum, leaving its quickly evolving reality to be defined by a toxic mix of ignorance, self-interest and conspiracy pundits.

A view of Qingyang Port, Kunshan

Making Sense of It

China and Kunshan's economic accomplishments are formidable, but little of it will make any real sense unless you visit. The reality beneath the economic numbers can only be found when you understand the area, its history, culture, environment and people. Through introduction, interviews and case studies you will be given the views of those who made, and are making Kunshan. The premise is that, to comprehend China today, you need to see it through the eyes of the people who are creating it.

Chapter 2

What Kunshan Has to Offer

Kunqu opera, originating in Kunshan, is the art form from which all Chinese opera styles are derived.

No discussion of Kunshan's economic success will make sense unless you understand its history, culture and environment.

Forest Park—One of many free parks in Kunshan

First Impressions

Late November is at the end of the Kunshan crab season. The sweet freshwater crustacean beckons the faithful each fall to the picturesque seasonal eateries rimming the lakes and river towns. It is an ancient migration, probably as old as the local Stone Age artifacts, which attest to the area's antiquity. Fertile lands and abundant water have been the constants, even as the tides of history have brought change. When you leave the superhighways and toll booths behind, you will notice the even well-tended fields, leveled by millenniums of minders, merging seamlessly into the horizon. Like the moss on a Live Oak, the feeling of age and magic in Kunshan's unchanged fields and river towns is often palpable; but as you land at Shanghai's Hongqiao International Airport, this reality is hidden by the grey forms of concrete and steel, ubiquitous to China's urban superstructure.

Ancient and Modern

When in Kunshan you are constantly aware of the struggle between ancient and modern energies; sequences of empires and invaders, rural agriculture and urban manufacturing, a modern republic founded by idealism and governed by pragmatism, the needs and desires of the local people and the economic forces driving globalization.

The Lou River

Today, as in the past, Kunshan uses strategic planning, innovative approaches and hard work to find the opportunities in the swirling tides of seasonal and economic change.

In area it is a little less than a thousand square kilometers, it encompasses nine towns and villages, four special economic development zones and multiple waterways and lakes, which take up about a third of its landscape. It is a place of four seasons, at the outlet of the Yangtze River; a river which like an arterial vein stretches from the eastern slopes of the Himalayas, past the Three Gorges Dam to Kunshan and Shanghai, delivering water and opportunity.

History

Pre-Republic

In 2003, the government reported that archeologists had discovered 10 paddy fields in northern Kunshan that were over 6,000 years old. They are the oldest paddy fields ever found in Yangtze River Delta, 3,000 years older than those found in Tokyo, Japan. The organization and complexity of the paddy fields indicate that south Suzhou was probably one of the earliest places where human beings develo-

13

ped intensive farming techniques. It gives you a sense of how ancient and settled this land is. It is a stark contrast to the vast wilderness from which the US was carved out over the last 350 years.

Interview with Mr. Chen Yi, Cultural History Scholar

Mr. Chen Yi is a noted local cultural scholar who is currently Academic Director of Kunshan's Cultural Development Research Center. For Mr. Chen who is 61 years old, the history of New China is in essence a description of his own life. When he was young life was hard, but it became even harder during the "cultural revolution"(1966-1976). Afterwards he worked in different cultural departments in Kunshan and devoted his spare time to writing a number of books about Kunshan's culture and history.

Q: What are the historical keys to understanding Kunshan?

A: For people outside of China, it is probably easiest for them to understand Kunshan if they understand the relationship between Kunshan and Shanghai. Kunshan was established as a county over 2,500 years ago. Shanghai was established 1,500 years later. Most of what is Shanghai today was administered by Kunshan before the Song Dynasty (960-1279). But, rather than being rivals we have always sought to share our benefits.

Shanghai although established later, developed faster. It grew rapidly as a trade center during the Song Dynasty (960-1279), and has since then used its geographic advantages and trade expertise to enlarge its economy. Kunshan although established first developed second, it was not until the mid 1980's that our modern economic face started to emerge. In Kunshan we believe what was once one thing can never really be divided and that the success and influences of one part will always eventually work to the benefit of the other.

Q: What has Kunshan contributed to China's history?

A: Much of Kunshan's contribution came during the Ming and Qing dynastyies (1368-1911). Shen Wansan, at the time, reputed to be the richest man in southern China, used Kunshan's geographical position in the Yangtze River Delta to create a thriving pioneer international trade business. The three famous wise men of Kunshan Gu Yanwu, Gui Youguang and Zhu Bolu developed new standards of teaching, style and philosophy which changed the face of China. They also left a strong moral legacy which stressed courage, practicality, directness and service which are the building blocks of what has become the Kunshan Way today. Like many things in China Kunshan's development was often dictated by events and directives created elsewhere, but the people have remained true to their ancestors' values and beliefs. The "opening up" gave us a stage and we have done our best to play our role.

Q: As a cultural scholar do you have any opinions about the future Kunshan?

A: The older generations who led China suffered a lot and lost time. The younger generations have had better living conditions and more opportunities but they face the challenge of preserving the essential parts of traditional Chinese culture. The influences of Western ideas and culture have helped China and some changes are inevitable but if we lose what makes us Chinese we will have paid too high a price.

Personally I am optimistic about traditional culture as I believe that as we develop socially and economically people will be more and more interested in preserving our traditional culture, because it defines who we are as a nation. As an example, I have been encouraged by the renewed interest young people have developed in some of our great philosophers and writers like Confucius and Lao Tse (Lao Tzu, or Lao Zi). Who would have predicted that a generation raised on video games would be so interested in the wisdom of the ancients. I am also encouraged by the efforts our government has made in protecting traditional culture like Kunqu Opera, but there is still a lot of work to be done.

My sense is that the value of a place is more than its economic advantages and that the values of the people and traditions are the defining element which separates places and makes one more attractive than another. For instance, whether you appreciate Kunqu Opera as an entertainment form, is separate from understanding its value as a cultural treasure. In the end the things we value and act on are the things that define us. Our reverence for the ideas of our ancestors and our actions today will be what makes Kunshan different and attractive to those who share similar values tomorrow.

Kunshan's Forefathers

Every place has its local heroes who represent the positive values that inspire its people. In the US we had George Washington, Thomas Jefferson, Benjamin Franklin, Abraham Lincoln, etc. Among the notable people who have shaped the character and beliefs of Kunshan's people are three wise men, an ancient millionaire and a modern genius.

Gu Yanwu

Gu Yanwu (1613-1682), also known as Gu Tinglin, was a famous Chinese philosopher, linguist, geographer and economist. From a wealthy Jiansu family, he spent his youth studying the classics and preparing for the civil service exams. The war which ended the Ming and created the Qing Dynasty also changed his life. As a solider he witnessed and felt the brutality of war, as his mother, step-mother, friends and neighbors were sacrificed to the desires of others for power and wealth. As a result, he devoted himself to anti-Manchu activities which however failed to return the Ming court to power, disillusioned with the realities of power and politics, he traveled the country and devoted himself to his studies. Despite numerous offers he consistently refused to serve the Qing Dynasty.

Gu was the first one to divide the rhymes of Old Chinese into 10 groups, based on the special phonological system of Old Chinese. His positivist approach to a variety of disciplines, and his criticism of Neo-Confucianism had a huge influence on later scholars. His works include *Yinxue Wushu (Five Works on Phonology)*, *Rizhi Lu (Records of Daily Knowledge)* and *Zhaoyu Zhi (Annals of the Land of China)*. He's also famous for the motto "Everybody is responsible for the fate of his country!"

Gu Yanwu—"Everybody is responsible for the fate of his country!"

His teachings and belief that the highest duty is to serve is still followed by his Kunshan descendants today. His famous quote was mentioned in five of the interviews as one of the guiding philosophies which defined their lives and actions. His influence actually goes far beyond just Kunshan, his words have been quoted by numerous national leaders, and they represent one of the philosophical pillars of Chinese society that the individuals' efforts are the bricks upon which the nation stands, "Country first, family second, self third."

Gui Youguang

Gui Youguang (1506-1571), one of the foremost stylists of the pure and lucid classical writing school of prose in the Ming Dynasty. Born to a wealthy family in Kunshan and educated in the Confucian classics, Gui's official career was undistinguished: he repeatedly failed the Imperial Examination and was only elevated to "official" status when he was almost sixty. By then, he had already achieved fame as a writer and teacher. He was said to have had several thousand students. As a famous prose author, his main achievement was the creation of a new writing style which was more direct, natural, as opposed to the self-involved emotional writing styles of the Tang and Song dynasties. "Xiangji Xuan Zhi", one of his most famous lyric prose, expressed his remembrance and love to his grandmother, mother and wife by describing all the daily routines and changes that happened in a small room called Xiangji Xuan in the old house of his family. His achievements should not be underestimated, in China, changes in style and philosophy often took centuries to be accepted, although it sounds simple what he was able to achieve in lifetime was singular. For the people of Kunshan his legacy has been the courage and belief that simple and direct ways will always be welcome.

Gui Youguang—Direct and practical stylist

Zhu Bolu

Zhu Bolu (1627-1698), a moralist and educator, was a native of Yushan in Kunshan. Like Gu Yanwu, the fall of the Ming Dynasty became the defining moment of his life. Like Gu Yanwu he lost a parent, his father, to the war in 1645. Because of the war he devoted the rest of his life to the study of ethics and philosophy. After the war Zhu came back to his hometown and began his career as an educator. Critical of the popular education models of the time, which were not practical or useful for teaching students, he wrote his own textbooks and curriculums. The main philosophy of his education was to call on people to be thrifty, caring and self-disciplined. His textbooks and methods soon became the accepted methodology for primary education in the Qing Dynasty. His book *Zhu Zi Jia Xun (Zhu's Family Instruction)* is considered classic in the area of ethics. Most importantly Zhu led by example and practiced what he preached. He devoted himself to the work which he thought was most useful. His resolve was apparent in his numerous rejections of honors and offers of promotion from the Qing Government.

Zhu's personal integrity was also mentioned as a guiding light, especially by the senior government officials I talked to.

Zhu Bolu—Educator and ethicist

Shen Wansan

Shen Wansan was a noble who lived towards the end of the Yuan Dynasty and the beginning of the Ming Dynasty. He was one of China's greatest and earliest international traders.

His history is shrouded in legend but it is undisputed that he became the richest man of his times. Historians believe that he relied on three factors:

Shen's father was a successful farmer and increased his land holdings by reclaiming areas from the marshes and lowlands that dominated the landscape. Shen continued his father's work and developed his first fortune.

After establishing himself, Shen used his talents and capital to expand his wealth. His empire quickly grew in two directions, agriculture and trade. He continued to reclaim land and used the Yangtze River system, as a distribution and logistics center, to sell Jiangsu and Zhejiang's silk, ceramics, food and handcraft products domestically and internationally.

The Yuan Dynasty, ruled by the descendants of Genghis Khan, had through their extensive conquests, opened trade routes and opportunities to the north and west. Shen took advantage of the times to establish an international trading empire. His money houses (banks) provided venture and expansion capital for the merchants whose goods he bought allowing him to concentrate on developing the logistics of his shipping empire.

Wealth and power are inseparable, in Shen's case his wealth brought him to the attention of Emperor Zhu Yuanzhang, founder of the Ming Dynasty. As a new emperor he had many reasons to fear and desire Shen's wealth. Through a series of pretexts he forced Shen to become a soldier in his army, confiscated his fortune and massacred over 80 of his family members. Some of Shen's sons survived and although they never rose to the heights their father did they used their knowledge of finance to lead very comfortable lives.

On the left:
Songmao Hall—The Shen Wansan house in
Zhouzhuang

Shen's family home, built by Shen Wansan's descendants, is located in Zhouzhu-ang Town. The well-preserved ancient residential house sits in the midst of elegant water views. Zhouzhuang Town is a magical place whose colorful local traditions and customs have earned it the nickname the "Venice of the East." Built in 1742 and located at the southeast side of Fu'an Bridge, the whole architectural complex is of the Qing's style and occupies an area of more than 2,000 square meters (half an acre). Over 100 rooms are divided into three sections and each one is connec-ted by arcades and aisles. The first is the water gate and the wharf, where Shen's family moored boats and washed clothes. The middle part includes the gate tower, the tearoom and the main hall. Brick gate towers, carved with lively and ingenious figures, depict historic stories and good wishes. The tearoom and main hall were places for serving guests, and the furnishings have been recreated to their original graceful style. The last section is the two-storied dwelling which consists of seve-ral parts that are quite different from the main hall, more comfortable and refined in pattern and atmosphere. For a glimpse of Shen Wansan you can see a painted sculpture of this legendary Kunshan forefather in the nearby Datang Tower.

Shen lives on in the memories of people in Kunshan as an example of ingenuity and enterprise, who used his talents to create great wealth. Like many of the sons of Kunshan he got caught in the tides of change.

An Wang

There is one more native of Kunshan who has a more modern success story. An Wang, a native of Kunshan, who was educated in the US, was the founder of Wang Laboratories. A brilliant researcher, with degrees from Shanghai-based Jiaotong University and the US's Harvard University, his company was the first to develop a useable computerized word processing system, which initially dominated the market.

Unfortunately, due to management problems the company declined relative to its competitors. In his later years Wang devoted his time to philanthropic projects including creating research facilities.

While every area in China has its famous citizens, Kunshan's seem to have a com-mon theme, that talent, hard work and a willingness to sacrifice can create future success and a better society.

Kunqu actress—Tinglin Park

Culture

Kunshan has a rich cultural heritage which includes its Stone Age settlements, ancient water towns, traditional foods, special flowers, precious stones, art museums and Kunqu Opera (or Kunshan Opera, a 600-year-old art form from which all Chinese opera styles, including Peking Opera, were derived.) There are things you need to do if you want to understand Kunshan's cultural history. You must go to a Kunqu opera, visit a water town, see the treasures of Tinglin Park, try the local foods and spend an afternoon appreciating the local tea culture.

Kunqu Opera

Of all its ancient cultural offerings, Kunqu Opera is what Kunshan is known for.

Kunqu's 600-year continuous history includes four distinct phases: a 200-year development stage, a 200-year golden age, a 200-year decline and a rebirth which started after the founding of the People's Republic of China (PRC).

The development period

The Kunshan Diao (Kunshan melody) was one of five major melodies in South Chinese theatre in late Yuan Dynasty (about 600 years ago). Mr. Wei Mingfu (1489-1566), a musician in the mid-Ming period, modified the Kunshan melody and combined it with some features of northern theatre. Consequently, Kunqu Opera was formed. Renowned for its gentle and clear vocals, beautiful and refined tunes, it gradually spread from Kunshan to nearby Suzhou and then the rest of China where it eventually became the dominant Chinese performance genre from the late Ming (1500s) to mid-Qing (1700s).

The Golden Age

Favored by the nobility, Kunqu Opera became a status symbol event. With more than 1,000 professional Kunqu actors around Suzhou alone, the talent pool was large and competitive. Most worked for public performing groups, while the best were recruited by wealthy families who used their private opera troupes to entertain themselves and their guests. If you were having a grand banquet, Kunqu Opera was essential. Banquets could last for over 10 hours, during which there would often be continuous opera performances.

During the reign period of Emperor Qianlong (1711-1799), Kunqu Opera reached its peak. In Suzhou there were 47 performing groups, and shows ran all year. Almost half of the children in Kunshan joined drama schools to be professional actors. The popularity of Kunqu Opera transcended differences of education, economics and

Kunqu Opera Museum and outdoor theatre—Tinglin Park

Mu Dan Ting(Peony Pavilion)—Kunqu Opera's most famous drama

class. It was even immortalized in Chinese writing where it was one of the running themes described in the Chinese classic *A Dream of Red Mansions*, by Cao Xueqin.

From the 1500s to the 1700s, 200 consecutive yearly Mid-Autumn Opera Festivals were held in Suzhou's Huqiu Hill. Every year over 10,000 Kunqu fans gathered there to watch the spectacle and decide by popular acclaim who the leading talents were.

The Decline

Although Kunqu Opera was widely appreciated, its flowery lyrics, slow tempo and historical symbolism were, for some, an acquired taste. It was also an expensive and time-consuming passion. Over time, Kunqu Opera became more of a special occasion, as opposed to a weekly entertainment. Tastes changed and more new accessible forms of opera developed. These new forms were referred to as "fickle opera" as opposed to Kunqu Opera which was referred to as "elegant opera."

Emperor Qianlong was so unhappy with the popularity of other operas that he ordered that all "fickle opera" shows be banned in Beijing. His attempts ultimately failed as the "fickle opera" continued to evolve in response to popular demand, while Kunqu Opera remained beautiful but static. It marked the beginning of Kunqu's decline. Peking Opera, which was developed based on Kunqu Opera, soon became the favorite of people in northern China, including the royal family and

Empress Cixi. By 1920s, there was only one small authentic Kunqu Opera performing group called Quan Fu Ban in southern China. Eventually it was forced to disband by the war and a lack of financial support.

Rebirth

In 1921, Zhang Zidong, a scholar from Suzhou, fearful that Kunqu would be lost forever, organized a group of twelve to raise funds for what became the Kunqu Transmission Institute. In August 1921, the institute began selecting students between the ages of 9 and 14. By 1922, 50 students were admitted after spending half a year probationary period to judge their talent and dedication, each one was asked to sign a formal five-year contract (three years of study, two years of performance).

These 50 people then carried on Kunqu until New China was founded in 1949. After the founding of the People's Republic, a number of artists started to use the Kunqu format to create new operas which had nationalistic themes. Their attempts met with approval both from the government and the local audiences. The most successful performance took place in 1956. *Shi Wu Guan (Fifteen Strings of Coins)*, a new Kunqu Opera show developed from an old story centering on concepts of "anti-subjectivism" and "anti-bureaucracy", was greeted warmly by central government leaders, including Chairman Mao Zedong and Premier Zhou Enlai. Premier Zhou Enlai had a 50-minute face-to-face talk with the performers after watching the show. Chairman Mao was so impressed he told the Minister of Culture: "This is a good show; it should be encouraged; it should be promoted nationwide."

With support from the authorities, Kunqu gained a new lease of life. *Shi Wu Guan* was being staged all over the country, at one point there were more than 60 performing groups which were performing the show in Zhejiang Province alone. Following its success, with the support of the Ministry of Culture and provincial governments, seven additional Kunqu Opera performing groups and institutes were founded over the following years. In 2000, the first Kunqu Opera Festival was held in Suzhou. In 2001, Kunqu Opera was listed as one of the Masterpieces of the Oral and Intangible Heritage of Humanity by UNESCO. In 2004, Mr. Bai Xianyong created a new Kunqu Opera show, *Mu Dan Ting (Peony Pavilion)*, which blended the traditional with the modern in an attempt to cater to young people's taste, which became successful.

There were over 360 regional opera styles which developed in China over 600 years, of which Kunqu Opera is regarded as one of the oldest and most influential. In 2008 Kunqu Opera was chosen as one of the performances for the opening ceremony of the Summer Olympics. At present, with less than 1,000 practitioners and less than 500 professional actors, Kunqu Opera is still struggling to reestablish itself.

Mr. Yang Shousong—Author of Kunqu Opera Road

Interview with Mr. Yang Shousong

Mr. Yang Shousong just published the *Kunqu Opera Road* in 2009. In addition to being an authority on Kunqu Opera, he is a reporter and author who has been honored twice nationally and once provincially for his work. Born in Yancheng, Jiangsu in December, 1943, he graduated from Nanjing University in 1968 (Chinese). His first job was as a secretary in the then Kunshan County Government. Please note that in China being a secretary is not the same as in the West. A secretary in China is an extension of their boss and acts as a high-level executive assistant.

In 1987, he was appointed as chairman of the county's federation of literary and art circles.

Two of his books, *Kunshan Road* in 1990 and *Suzhou Fellow Townsman* in 1992 had a huge impact on people's discussions and ideas about the "opening-up" process.

Q: What should foreigners know about Kunqu Opera?

A: Kunqu Opera is one of the oldest forms of Chinese opera. It evolved from the Kunshan Diao, a melody which served as the basis for the initial songs used in the operas. Chinese Opera is a traditional form of Chinese theatre combining dialogue, music, vocal performance, dance, Kungfu, acrobatics and highly stylized and expressive make-up and acting. Along with Sanskrit Opera and Greek Theatre, it is one of the three oldest living theatrical art forms in the world. The origin of Chinese Opera, like Western theatre, traces its beginnings back to primitive songs and dances associated with religious ceremonies.

Q: It seems that Kunqu Opera is struggling to adapt and still be true to its ancient traditions. What is the future of Kunqu Opera?

A: There are two schools of thought: one holds that Kunqu Opera should not change but maintain its status as a living piece of intangible heritage; and the other school believes that Kunqu Opera will only survive if it adapts itself as it has in the past to be relevant. Personally I believe both.

Author's Note

Like many things in China and Kunshan, the desire to preserve the past is sometimes seemingly at odds with the dynamics of a changing world. Kunqu Opera may not be something that we in the West can readily appreciate, but if you get the chance to see a performance while sitting in one of the open-air courtyards, take it. It is a rare opportunity to glimpse a living piece of history and be part of a 600-year-old tradition. Like Western opera, to fully appreciate Kunqu Opera you need to know and understand the stories, symbolism and the incredible training which its practitioners master. If you are serious, a little preparation might be in order; if not, just pretend you are Marco Polo at an imperial entertainment.

In addition to an introduction to Kunqu, I was taken to meet a group of primary school children from Kunshan No.1 Primary School and watch them go through their paces under the watchful eyes of professional Kunqu Opera masters. It was a free Saturday program which is also offered at other schools in the area. Roughly forty children from the ages of 8 to 15 participated in an energetic series of exercises. One of a number of school programs it is one of the intangible heritage preservation efforts China has developed to save its cultural past. I thought it would be interesting to interview the children to see how they viewed their role in this national effort.

The long road to perfection

Interview with Three Young Kunqu Opera Students (Girls)

Zhong (9 years), Shu (11 years), Shen (11 years)

Q: How long have you been studying Kunqu Opera?

A: We have been learning Kunqu Opera for three years.

Q: Do you like it? Do you want to be a Kunqu Opera actress?

A (Zhong): It's helped my singing and I am doing better in my studies. My dream is to be both a Kunqu Opera star and a movie actress.

A (Shu): I was recruited to come to the Kunqu Opera class, and my parents approved. My favorite part is the singing.

A (Shen): I also like singing the most.

Q: What do you think is the most interesting part for foreigners to appreciate Kunqu Opera?

Kunqu Opera students—Old traditions new students

The apprentice

A (Shu): For foreigners, the most interesting part of Kunqu Opera is martial arts.

Q: Do you feel it's unfair that most of your friends are able to rest and enjoy watching TV and playing video games at home each weekend?

A (Zhong): I feel it's more interesting to come to class than staying at home and play video games. My physical fitness is better and I can do lots of tricks. There are also lots of performing opportunities and awards.

Interview with Two Young Kunqu Opera Students (Boys)

Junping and Junhui (twins)

Q: How long have you been studying Kunqu Opera and what's your favorite part?

A: We have been studying Kunqu Opera for three years and we both like the singing the best.

Q: Your relationship with each other as twins?

A: We are close but we fight a lot.

Q: What's the job you dream of in the future?

A (Junping): I hope to be a pop singer.

A (Junhui): I want to be a Kunqu Opera actor.

Q: How do you like the classes?

A: Training in Kunqu Opera helps our physical development. We are more flexible and healthy and the martial arts can be fun and useful.

Q: Are your friends interested in Kunqu Opera?

A: Some are, and others think it's very boring.

Author's Note

It will be interesting to see if a new style of pop music which uses Kunqu Opera influences is evolved in the future. I was told that Kunqu Opera stars are already crossing over into music and acting fairly successfully.

Water Towns

Zhouzhuang

Zhouzhuang, China's most stunning water town, where ancient buildings flank rivers crisscrossed by stone bridges. To appreciate it, sit in a teahouse and let the afternoon slip away while you talk to friends and sample the snacks which come with your tea. Take the time to learn how to select, make and appreciate tea, understand why it is a cultural activity. As the small wooden boats pass by, you will have a glimpse into a way of life which has changed little in 1,000 years. It will give you new insights into the beautiful houses of Kunshan's famous families, their formal reception halls, endless courtyards, secret escape routes and hidden gardens, where Chinese noble families practiced tea culture as a way of life.

Ms.Anna Kajumulo Tibaijuk, Under-Secretary-General of the United Nations and Executive Director of the United Nations Human Settlements Program (UN-HABITAT), visits Zhouzhuang

Zhouzhuang is located in Kunshan, it is less than an hour's bus or car ride from the centers of Kunshan, Shanghai and Suzhou. Temperatures range from -5ºC in January, the coldest month, to a high of 36ºC in July. Since the city wears the time of day and the seasons like a sequence of beautiful robes, every time you go will be memorable.

Although many people go for a day trip, the best way is to spend a day or two, come in the late afternoon, walk the town and have a leisurely dinner. Spend the night in a restored mansion or local house, or in one of the more conventional nearby hotels. If you rise early you can experience the city as the sun rises and its empty streets become a post card of the past. You need to experience Zhouzhuang, connect with the local pace of life and experience its cultural wonders, not just admire its beauty. Wander along the rivers, either by foot or gondola, and you will be engulfed by its ancient Ming and Qing dynasty architecture, carefully preserved by the local government. Watch Kunqu Opera in the same style Chinese nobles

Zhouzhuang—China's most beautiful waterside town

enjoyed, visit the local teahouse and restaurants, taste the local specialties and shop the local bamboo and bronze handicrafts. Zhouzhuang is a real town, not an ersatz Disneyland, but it has a new role as a cultural ambassador of China's past, a role which protects China's priceless heritage and provides new economic opportunities for its residents.

On the right:
Ancient paved roads in Qiandeng

Qiandeng Town

Qiandeng Town is another water town which was developed a little later than Zhouzhuang. It is the hometown of famous philosopher Gu Yanwu and earliest Kunqu Opera composer Gu Jian. Its ancient stone buildings, temples, museums, and courtyard houses also provide a glimpse into China's past. With so many years of history each town has its legends and stories. Qiandeng picturesque gates and central bell tower testifies to its past importance and its role as a trading city. The commercial drive is still visible today as its bustling streets resonate with the sounds of vendors and customers engaged in the day-to-day supply and demand. It is a place where the past and present of China meet. Old buildings and new vendors are juxtaposed against China's ancient culture and its modern direction. The two interviews I had, one with a hard-working family of vendors and another with a young tour guide, had one thing in common, a shared belief that under China's current direction, all you need is an idea, hard work and a little luck and the future will be bright; ironically the same values which at one time propelled the "American Dream". If the ability to create hope is one of the measures of a society's success then Kunshan, China is succeeding. It also indicates that China's national/city model is a working system which should be studied more closely.

Qiandeng—Where local food and heritage meet

Mr. Tian and Ms. Zhang, Qiandeng Town store vendors

Mr. Tian and Ms. Zhang (couple) are owners of the Ke Xin Qing Grocery Store in Qiandeng Town. They make their own products and rent their stall from private owners. They work 7 days a week starting at 5 am and finishing at 8 pm. Originally from Heilongjiang they moved when their clothing business was no longer profitable. She thinks the local economy is better and the local people are more businesslike. Her son owns another stall in another part of Qiandeng Town. They were doing a brisk business on a cold and blustery day. She did most of the talking and made it clear that things are much better now than they were before and she expects things to continue to improve.

Mr. Tian and Ms. Zhang are part of Kunshan's migrant economy which includes labors, construction workers and legions of small businesses. Working together 105 hours a week is their choice but it also explains why China's economy is able to make such massive strides. The US in earlier times had a similar work ethic and drive and it allowed us to surpass our European rivals. Unsurprisingly it seems the tables may have turned.

Mrs. Cheng (Tour guide in Qiandeng Town)

Born in Henan, with relatives in Kunshan, she has been working for the Qiandeng Tour Group for five years. She majored in tourism and believes Qiandeng is changing rapidly in a positive direction. Over the last couple of years, she thinks government economic policies have had positive impact, most people's lives are improving quickly. People have more business opportunities and are able to buy luxuries as well as necessities. She works 6 days a week from 8 am to 5 pm, or as needed. Married, she has one child. She expects that her fourteen-month-old daughter will have more opportunities than she and her husband had. She likes flowers and is looking forward to the Shanghai Expo where Qiandeng will have a booth. She has noticed that Qiandeng is being used more and more as a movie and TV show location and hopes it will continue.

One of the differences between the US and China is, while we have developed technology, manufacturing, logistics, distribution, marketing and financial systems, China has people like Mr. Tian, Ms. Zhang and Mrs. Cheng, who seem willing to work, in what we would consider brutal hours, for what they believe is a better future. In our earlier history we had the same determination and drive and it propelled us past our European rivals. Today we have different expectations but we should not be surprised when those who are willing to put the time in and get results. So when you are in Kunshan, or any other part of China, it might be worth getting to know the reality behind the facts. It will at least begin to give you an idea of how China is able to do what it does.

On the right:
Jinxi, home to Chinese folk museums

The Treasures of Tinglin Park

A pleasant way of getting to know Kunshan's history and culture is to visit Tinglin Park. Located in the middle of Kunshan's main town it offers the "Three Treasures" of Kunshan: Kunshan Stone, Jade Flower, and Twin-lotus Flower, along with museums, a Kunqu Opera House, Kunshan's highest scenic spot Jade Peak and a glimpse of a vibrant local community in action.

Kunshan Stone

Kunshan stone is one of the "four noble stones" of China which are prized by collectors, the other three are Lingbi Stone (quarried in Anhui Province), Taihu Lake Stone (Jiangsu Province) , and Yingde Stone (Guangdong Province). The stone has been quarried for thousands of years from Yufeng Mountain (Jade Peak) which sits in the middle of Tinglin Park. Formed over millions of years by geological and volcanic action, it has very high hardness and purity (91.57% silicon dioxide), which is close to that of agate, under a microscope you can see a matrix of crossing crystalline structure. Unfortunately it is also very brittle, which makes it hard to process. Most are stand-alone pieces.

The stone comes in a number of varieties and is enjoyed for its colors and natural delicacy: Lotus Leaf Crease, honeycombed Anthill Peak, super-thin Chicken-bone Peak, crystalline Snow-white Peak are some of the names given. The collectable value has increased markedly as the people's disposable income and interest in collectables has increased. In terms of supply, since Jade Peak's mines were shut down by the government to preserve it, the supply has been cut off. Lotus Leaf Crease, for example, can sell for ten times its weight in gold.

Jade Flower

The Jade Flower is a rare "living fossil" found only in China. The biggest single plant grows in Tinglin Park. It flowers from mid-April to mid-May, but its perennially changing hues are an exquisite kind, making it a feast for the eyes, even when not in bloom.

Kunshan Stone—Kunshan's most precious stone

The Jade Flower—Symbol of longevity and beauty

Twin-lotus flower

Twin-lotus Flower

Legend has it that the Twin-lotus Flower was introduced into China from India. A Yuan Dynasty poet Gu A'ying through careful breeding developed flowers in multiple configurations with buds facing apart, or clustered tightly together. They became known as the East Pavilion Lotus because the poet's garden was in East Pavilion Village of Zhengyi Town. When they bloom they spread their perfume across the park and their blossoms offer another breathtaking part of Tinglin Park.

The Community

If you can, go in the morning and watch the sun rise. You will be greeted by a cross section of the community which uses the park as their daily social and exercise club. Young children with their parents, retired locals and school children walk the ancient paths to the museums and attractions, activity areas and nature trails. It is an extraordinary sight to see: people singing Kunqu Opera, playing traditional instruments, practicing Kungfu, ballroom dancing, exercising and flying kites. Those not involved in physical activities use the benches and tables for Mahjong, Chinese chess, Go and casual chatting. Locals, children and retirees get in free or at reduced prices. According to my guide the park is one of those magical places where people bump into old friends and make new ones. Most importantly you get a sense of what China was and is when you take away the new buildings and busy streets.

Tinglin Park—Morning exercises

Food

Obviously, for most visitors, trying the local specialties is one of the most interesting and accessible ways of getting to know the local tastes and culture. In China food is more than nutrition, and hospitality, it is entertainment and a way of life. No matter where you go in China, if you can pry yourself away from the bland recreations of Western fare ubiquitous to multiple star hotels and the fast food joints, and try the local specialties you will be rewarded with a delicious and memorable adventure.

The best way to find the right restaurant and food is through the locals. They can steer you around the high-priced tourist traps to their favorite eateries and dishes. Be up front about what you like: hot, sweet, salty, sour, vegetarian, etc..., but be open to sampling things. If you want a Western-style bathroom say so, no one will be offended. Also there is no shame in taking a bite and then spitting it out on your plate if you don't like it. Just indicate that it does not suit your tastes and try something else.

The food in Kunshan ranges from delicacies like Yangcheng Lake Mitten Crabs to hearty staples like Aozao Noodles and Wansan Pork Shank. The ingredients and tastes are very accessible to most Western palates. In addition, Kunshan has an excellent selection of Taiwanese restaurants serving snacks and specialties.

To give you an idea of some things you might want to try and their history, I have listed some of the memorable culinary highlights which I tasted.

Tasting Yangcheng Lake crabs

Yangcheng Lake Chinese Mitten Crabs

Every autumn, the highway between Shanghai and Kunshan is jammed with the culinary faithful. Yangcheng Lake is a fresh-water body on the primary crab migration route to and from the Yangtze River. The clean, deep water, abundant vegetation and firm lake bed create a clean fleshy crab which is prized for its natural sweetness and delicate flavor.

You can get mitten crabs in many places in China, but Yangcheng Lake is acknowledged to offer the best. Part of the experience is savoring the juicy delicacies as you sit in a lakeside eatery enjoying the fresh breezes, channeled by the low, misty hills, and watch the sun setting over the horizon.

Bacheng Town, located northwest of Kunshan, on the shores of Yangcheng Lake, is the crab season gourmands' ground zero. With more than 1,000 restaurants, cooking crabs is a way of life. In fact most restaurants are only open for the crab season. They tend to be small family-run affairs, but there is a restaurant for every taste and budget. Within Bacheng there are four main districts. The traditional crab market is located on Hubin Road, where you can buy crabs directly from one of the hundred crab fisher boats that line up each day during the season. Bajie Road which is nearby attracts patrons willing to swap a sunset view and a water breeze for a more reasonably priced dinner.

The crabs are boiled and served with simple sauces, generally either vinegar or chili oil. Personally I prefer them plain and then use a small amount of vinegar to rinse off my fingers after the feast.

If you are looking for a gift which will always be appreciated, buy a box of crabs. They will gladly wrap them for you at the airport if you are traveling to other parts of China and you will be very warmly welcomed wherever you go.

Crab Tips

A few ways to tell if you are getting a real Yangcheng Lake Hairy Crab: ask to see the crabs before they are cooked. The tops should be a greenish blue with black tints which should turn bright red when cooked. The belly should be white and glossy, the claws should be golden-colored, shiny and surrounded by golden hairs (mittens). To tell if it is a male or female, look at the belly flap, males have elongated flaps while females have round ones. Locals believe that female crabs taste best in the ninth and males in the tenth month of the lunar calendar; the female's roe is firm and full and male fat is thick and solid during those times.

Crab eating is quite a delicate operation, with a set of eight "instruments", each dedicated to attacking a different part of the crab. Locals are happy to teach you the process. One thing they warned me not to do was eat the small part located in the middle of the body, as they believe it is bad for the stomach. I am not sure if I believe this but, given they have been eating these crabs for 10,000 years, it might be better to bow to local wisdom. Things to go with your crab include: Yellow wine, which is a tonic for the throat and warms your spirit, ginger tea with brown sugar, which warm your body and dried plums, which help with the seafood odors and digestion.

Ao Zao Mian (Noodles)

The locals say "you have not been to Kunshan unless you have eaten Aozao Noodles", and the best place for Aozao Noodles is the Aozao Restaurant on Tinglin Road, two blocks from Tinglin Park (It is the perfect place to stop before or after a visit). The plaque on door "Aozao Restaurant - Time-honored Store in China", is by the

The world-famous Aozao Noodles Restaurant

famous Chinese calligrapher and painter Song Wenzhi. The restaurant dates back to 1853, the 3rd year of Emperor Xian Feng, of the Qing Dynasty. I was puzzled as to how it survived the initial period of the New Republic and was informed that even in difficult times everyone wants delicious food.

The two-story restaurant itself is light and airy with numerous windows and high ceilings, a historical throwback to the times before the Republic of China. The large dining rooms buzz with the activity of families, friends and visitors enjoying food and fellowship.

After an initially rocky start the restaurant blossomed under the control of Madame Chen Xiuying who created a red sauce noodle dish which had people lining up. The thin pasta noodles served in a slightly savory red sauce, with sides of hot chili oil and fresh seasonings which you add as desired are aromatic, stylishly presented and mouth-wateringly delicious.

In terms of its past, there are many stories about how the noodles were named Aozao (Ao = profound or mysterious, Zao = stove). One story is that Emperor Qian Long (one of the most successful and highly respected statesmen in Chinese his-

tory), was so impressed by the taste of the Red Sauce Noodles that he instructed his servant to learn the secret of making the dish. Unfortunately because he could not speak the local dialect he was unable to get the recipe. Rather than admit failure he told the Emperor: "It's not about the process, but the place; the secret (Ao) of the dish is in their stoves (Zao)." As a result, the dish was referred to as Aozao Noodles.

Another version is that the restaurant's popularity drew the ire of its jealous competitors who tried to defame the popular noodle dish by calling it Ao Zao Mian (which means "foul noodles" in the local dialect). A well-known scholar, and regular customer, decided to turn the tables on the competitors by separating the two characters into Ao and Zao, creating a name which suggested a profound culinary experience.

While the past may be uncertain the present is not, today the Aozao Restaurant is a favorite of locals and visitors alike. In addition to the Red Rauce Noodles they have added White Sauce Noodles which are lighter and served in a duck stock. I would suggest trying both. In addition they offer locally smoked fish, hairy crabs, fresh-water shrimp and many of the other Kunshan delicacies described below.

It is particularly a great place to stop before or after visiting Tinglin Park which is only two blocks away.

Wansan Pork Shank

Wansan Pork Shank is considered one of the tastiest local dishes, it is named after Shen Wansan, who served it to his distinguished guests. But it is more than just food, it is food with a story as so often is the case in China.

The story has to do with the way the dish is served. Rather than cutting into it you simply remove the thin bone which runs the length of the pork shank, the meat is rendered ready to eat without having to disturb the outer skin. The story is that Emperor Zhu (Zhu sounds similar to the word for "pig" in Chinese) Yuanzhang, founder of the Ming Dynasty, was looking for some pretext to kill Shen Wansan and confiscate his lands and wealth. At a feast in his honor the Emperor asked Shen a tricky question "What's the name of this dish?" Shen knew that if he said "pig (zhu) shank" it could be construed as an insult to the Emperor who could then seize his wealth and imprison him, cleverly he said "This is my favorite, so it's called Wansan Pork Shank." The Emperor then asked, "How do you eat this Pork Shank?" The wily Shen knew that if he said "cut it up with knife", the Emperor would have had him instantly beheaded, since it could be interpreted to indicate that he would willingly cut up the meat of Zhu with a knife. Instead Shen suggested the novel bone removal method which saved his life.

The dish itself depends on careful material selection, only the center portion of choicest fresh Pork Shank is used, after being rubbed with spices and herbs it is simmered for an entire day until reddish brown and fragrant. The method of preparation renders the meat tender and non greasy.

A Po Tea (Granny's Tea)

A Po Tea is part of Kunshan's local tea culture: it does not refer to a specific kind of tea, but to a tradition of hospitality which has developed over thousands of years. Every detail, from the invitation to the snacks and the serving of the tea, is a formula which host and guest know and follow.

Beyond getting together and sharing a warm beverage, tea is a cultural activity. Kunshan's local tea culture includes Settlement Tea (for settlement of disputes, held in a public teahouse), Wedding Tea (held on the morning after the wedding ceremony), Spring Tea (held during the first 15 days of the lunar new calendar year), Full-Month Tea (celebrating the 30th or 40th day after a baby's birth), but A Po Tea (or Granny's Tea) is probably the most famous of all, as indicated by the saying that "A trip to Zhouzhuang is never complete without drinking A Po Tea".

A Po Tea is the formal way of expressing hospitality among neighbors, by hosting the tea you honor your guests who in turn honor you with their presence. Although it has a folksy name it has a sophisticated protocol. The host sets an auspicious date for the tea, then goes door to door to invite guests, the treasured old lovely blue and white tea sets are brought out and cleansed and traditional snacks are prepared. On the day of the tea, guests greet their hosts and drink tea while the hosts offer peeled fruits and snacks as a gesture of hospitality.

The tea is served by first filling the cup half way, then the tea is allowed to steep for a while before the cup is filled. This method is deemed as a gesture of honest hospitality. As a guest, you should not leave until your cup has been filled at least three times.

But, since you will probably not be lucky enough to be invited to a local A Po Tea the next best thing is a A Po Teahouse.

In Zhouzhuang the Echo Teahouse offers an A Po Tea. The Teahouse was named for Chen Maoping (Echo) (1943-1991), a Taiwanese writer who lived in and wrote about her life in Zhouzhuang. Mr. Zhang Jihan, the owner of this Teahouse, also a noted local author and former director of Zhouzhuang's Culture Committee, had invited Echo to revisit Zhouzhuang, but her return was prevented by her untimely death. The two-floor classic riverside teahouse, which bears her name, is decorated with the pictures and writings of the now silent Echo.

If you want to experience China's tea culture you need to bring friends and take your time. The experience is about enjoying tea, delicious snacks and friendship as you sit in the midst of ancient stone buildings by the slow-flowing river and the boats which ply it.

Some helpful tips: do not drink from the first brewing of the tea, use the tea to wash the cups and then start drinking from the second pot. Usually a selection of snacks will be brought with the tea, but I suggest ordering the entire menu and then sampling them one by one. Think of it as a leisurely English Cream Tea. Mr. Zhang recommends flaky bean curd, sunflower seeds, crisp fried beans and the small sweet cakes and candies made locally.

The best way to enjoy an A Po Tea is to come to Zhouzhuang in the late afternoon, have dinner, see the town as the light fades, stay at a riverside house or local hotel and then rise early in the morning and see it as the light reveals a new town. Stroll the streets, visit the museums and historical sites, try the local foods, shop the stalls and then enjoy a leisurely A Po Tea. It will change your sense of China and connect you with its past.

Qiandeng Lamb

Qiandeng lamb is locally raised lamb which is prized for its texture and taste. There are over 30 different local recipes which offer every variety of cooking method and combination. There are few things more tasty than sizzling lamb kebabs and cold local Tsingtao(Qingdao) beer. The agricultural park restaurants often offer wonderful selections and pleasant surrounding.

Zhoushi Duck

Zhoushi Duck is boiled then marinated in cloves, cinnamon fennel and Chinese herbs, it is then cooked quickly to keep the meat moist and the skin crispy. This traditional dish was developed by Kunshan farmers who hunted for ducks in the abundant waterways and marshlands of the area. Eaten by emperors and prized in Shanghai it is well worth tasting.

Sweet Green Rice Dumplings and Sock Sole Pastries

Sweet green rice dumplings and sock sole pastries are two local snack foods well worth tasting. The sweet green rice dumplings are made with specially flavored rice with a sweet bean filling and the sock sole pantries are delicate cakes named for their shape which are sprinkled with sweet and savory toppings.

Kunshan has also absorbed the flavors of its international residents and there are an excellent selection of restaurants serving foods from all over Asia and the world. If you are looking for ingredients there are a number of well-stocked international grocery stores which cater to every taste.

The hundred-year-old sweet green rice dumpling shop in Zhengyi

Locals singing Kunqu Opera in Tinglin Park

Entertainment

Kunshan is close to Shanghai's F1 Circuit, has its own 30,000-seat stadium, a 6,000-seat multi-purpose gymnasium, four international-grade golf courses, numerous agricultural parks, lakes, spas, and marinas. Many of its lakes, like Yangcheng and Dianshan, are a favorite vacation spot for those escaping the heat, humidity, traffic and pollution of Shanghai summers. You can buy or rent a modest cottage or a waterfront mansion depending on your tastes and budget. Kunshan's major attraction is its relaxed atmosphere, breathtaking ancient scenery, water activities and food.

"Enjoying life at every stage"

Kunshan has a number of notable museums which present the past as well as the future. One of the museums, the Hou Beiren Art Museum, has an interesting history which also illustrates the Kunshan Way. To get the story I talked to Mr. Zhao Zongkai, president and chief curator, Hou Beiren Art Museum. Mr. Zhao Zongkai, a painter, born in Shanghai, has worked in Kunshan for over 20 years, but while living in California, he became friends with Mr Hou Beiren, a famous Chinese artist whose works blend traditional and contemporary techniques and subjects. When he found out that his friend was looking for a museum to donate his works to, Mr. Zhao acted quickly. Although Liaoning, Beijing and Shanghai were interested, based on a report submitted by Mr. Zhao at 10 am the Kunshan government made a complete offer by 2 pm the same day. Mr. Hou Beiren was so impressed he immediately agreed. The deal resulted in a new museum whose permanent collection attracts hundreds of thousands of people each year. Built on a beautiful park (Langhuan Park) on the site of a former Party school, it is both a place of aesthetic interest and daily community activity.

Kunshan International Beer Festival

The Kunshan Exhibition Center, located opposite Kunshan's municipal square on

Qianjin Road, is also worth visiting. On the second floor you can see the timeline and products which have defined Kunshan's economic march. On the third floor there is a history and art museum which traces Kunshan's ancient and artistic accomplishments. Donated by Mr. Zhu Fuyuan, a noted businessman and art collector, who was born in Kunshan, but lives and works in Japan, it is an excellent venue to see the breadth of what Kunshan has accomplished economically and culturally.

The city has three major and countless neighborhood parks which serve as community social and exercise centers. While the days when thousands of bicycles made their twice daily pilgrimage, have been replaced by cars and electric bicycles, the daily routines and activities in the parks have remained. Old, young and everyone in between use the parks to chat and exercise in a daily symphony which is a show in itself. In addition to Tinglin Park, Forest and Bolu Parks are the main ones. If you are interested in what Kunshan people do and the rhythms of their lives, go to the parks and you will not be disappointed.

Not content with its current offerings, Kunshan is vigorously pursuing other entertainment attractions, including tourism festivals, sporting events, concerts and festivals. Its annual beer festival is already a huge attraction. Thousands of people descend each August and September to sample Oktoberfest in China.

Living Environment

Many cities in China have grown quickly without regard for their history or environment, creating unrelenting landscapes of concrete. Perhaps because of its cultural heritage and with an eye to the climbing economic value-added ladder, Kunshan has done better than most in creating an attractive and livable environment. Traditional structures and areas have been maintained and protected; tourists and locals are able to enjoy China's past, as well as the conveniences of an international city.

Demography

Dianshan Lake Resort

Kunshan is home to over 100,000 expatriates representing countries and regions from all over the world. The largest group is people from China's Taiwan Province who have brought their businesses, families, food, schools and health care facilities with them. In total almost 2 million people live in Kunshan, of whom about one third are registered residents and the rest are migrant workers and foreigners.

Shopping

While it can not compare to Shanghai, Kunshan has its share of Western department

Kunshan's newest sports and entertainment facility

and grocery stores like Wal-Mart. But, if you are looking for world-class shopping it is only a 20-minute train ride away in Shanghai. If you crave junk food or coffee, the local KFC's, McDonalds, Pizza Hut and Starbucks are ready to serve you.

In terms of the local population; on a daily basis you see crowds of people shopping, eating and enjoying life. Disposable incomes are relatively high. After a house and a car the main items of desire seem to be branded clothes and accessories, cell phones, computers and other electronic goods.

Housing

Housing prices are a third of Shanghai's. Housing types vary from detached houses to apartments and condos. The town while bustling is manageable, due to its well-kept roads and public transportation system. From Tinglin Park to the water towns of Zhouzhuang, Qiandeng and Jinxi, Kunshan offers a convenient city environment with an incredible mix of old and new China.

Education

Kunshan has two schools which cater to international students. In addition, it has an excellent local education system which gets more than its fair share of students into the best schools in China. As this is one of the major areas of concern to families looking at Kunshan, it is an area which the government is looking closely at.

Over the past 5 years Kunshan has led the nation in attracting new institutions of higher education and its aggressive research and development strategy has already led to joint projects with some of the best institutions from home and abroad like Tsinghua University, China and Duke University in the US.

Riverside apartments

on the left:
Hou Beiren Art Museum

Investing in the future, the Kunshan Children's Activity Center

Zhenchuan High school

A new season for a new generation

Chapter 3
The Kunshan Way

New paths across old fields

The Kunshan Way describes how a city, which 20 years ago ranked last in its area, rose from a largely agricultural county to become the most successful county-level city in China.

Through a number of interviews you will see how the Kunshan Way developed, the components of the Kunshan Way, how those strategies are implemented, the role economic development zones (EDZs) play and how its urban economic success is affecting its rural constituents. Kunshan is a microcosm of some of the best trends and developments in China.

Xiajiayuan New Type of Rural Community

Its history, strategies, tools and successes are models which need to be understood. While not complete, the Kunshan Way is a new economic development methodology which is changing the norms and roles of economic development, the same way Japanese production concepts changed the manufacturing world 30 years ago. Whether you are competing with or in China, you need to understand what the Kunshan Way is.

Please note, in the US cities are urban by definition, but in China cities are more like organizational units. They are responsible for the lands and people in their areas, whether urban or rural. This distinction should not be overlooked as it reflects a profound difference in the roles and responsibilities of cities and leaders in the US and China. Given that most people are one generation or less removed from their agricultural roots, the always present specter of 800 million farmers waiting in the wings and China's socialist ideology; rural issues are never far from the agenda.

Also keep in mind that Chinese and US cities differ drastically in their structure

Going green

and leadership mechanisms. US cities are independent entities run by elected officials who use appointed functionaries to manage the civil servants who operate the mechanics of government. Chinese cities are run by largely appointed officials who manage a civil service corps of mainly Party members whose priorities are set in Beijing. This central planned economy focus has been one of the major driving forces behind China's recent economic success and perhaps its major competitive advantage vs. Western economies; but it is only one part of the equation which also needs to be understood at the implementation level.

China still uses the system of five-year economic plans, but unlike the system which failed the USSR, the Chinese under Deng adapted their planning process to be more pragmatic; to emphasize finding solutions rather than imposing them. As former Party Secretary Wu Kequan of Kunshan observed, economic development is both a chess game and a field sport, planning is vital but it is not a substitute for implementation and vice versa.

As you read through the dialogs with Kunshan's government leaders you will notice that much of their success is based on their ability to work "within the box," to create new implementation solutions which follow the central government's directives. The dialogs with the various Party and government leaders are designed to give you a sense of Kunshan's economic history, strategy and implementation methods.

While rural issues in China often take second seat to economic issues, they are probably the best measure for how well the city is operating. So in addition to talking to people at the top of the power structure, I have included interviews with rural residents whose perspective on change offers a second measure of Kunshan's success.

History

It would be hard to separate the rise of Kunshan and Mr. Wu Kequan, the former Party secretary of Kunshan. Over the couple of days I had the privilege of chatting with him, I learned that the true strength of China's economic system is the people, their intelligence ethics and dedication.

As discussed in detail later on, China's internal government structure is based on a top-down series of management units which include: provinces and major municipalities, sub-provincial cities and provincial capitals, prefecture-level cities, county-level cities, townships, villages, and collectives.

There are also a number of special administrative and autonomous regions which are outside the normal structure.

Twenty years ago, Kunshan County became a county-level city. By moving up, it was able to qualify for more flexible economic development tools which it has used to create its current economic success. Mr. Wu Kequan was the first Party secretary of Kunshan City and was responsible for creating many of the approaches and concepts which define the Kunshan Way.

Interview with Mr. Wu Kequan

Mr. Wu's Background

Tea and conversation with Mr. Wu Kequan

- 1955-1961, National Planning Commission;
- 1961-1981, Gansu Provincial Planning Commission;
- 1981, Vice-mayor, Kunshan Township (became Mayor in 1984);
- 1984, New Industrial Park created (recognized at the national level as Kunshan Economic and Technological Development Zone ,or KETD for short, in 1992);
- 1989, The first Kunshan City Party Secretary after Kunshan Township was promoted to a county-level city;
- 1991, Vice-chairman of Standing Committee of People's Congress of Suzhou City;
- 1994, Vice-Party Secretary of the China-Singapore Suzhou Industrial Park (a joint venture between the government of Singapore and China and the most successful development zone in China);
- 1998 Retired and lives in Kunshan.

Q: Why has Kunshan been so successful?

A: Our proximity to Shanghai has given us a geographical advantage. The policies and approaches Deng Xiaoping advocated, 30 years ago, created the starting point. The national policy of "opening up" created a new era not only in substance but also in tone. Instead of complex ideological slogans Deng gave us simple but powerful models of how we should think about our efforts. For example, "It doesn't matter if a cat is black or white, so long as it catches mice"("Deng Xiaoping Anthology") helped us understand that using capitalist mechanisms to advance socialist principles was acceptable; "Seek truth from facts"("Deng Xiaoping Anthology") encouraged us to rely on empirical rather than theoretical approaches in our efforts. "Crossing the river by feeling for stones"("Deng Xiaoping Anthology") made us aware of the need to be pragmatic when pursuing our goals. Together with careful study, pragmatic approaches, consistent hard work and help from others, we were able to achieve some successes. I want to stress that we have always understood that past successes do not create future ones and it is what has motivated us to keep up the level of our efforts.

The "opening up" period also ushered in other important changes which affected the roles and responsibilities of the different levels of government. Having worked for the Planning Commission, both at the national and provincial levels, for me it was clear that central planning had its strengths and limitations. Deng's ideas were methods rather than answers. To follow his ideas, we had to switch from following formulas to finding the solutions that fit the situation. As areas differ, cities found themselves increasingly at the frontline of the effort to implement the central government's policies at the local level. Based on the success of the system, the central government started managing more by objective, where innovative solutions which advanced the country's goals were valued and often adopted.

Q: How did this change in thinking affect Kunshan?

A: Kunshan is part of the Yangtze River Delta, an area that has been important in terms of trade and government for millenniums. But by 1979 the area had retreated to a primarily agrarian economy. For the first ten years after "opening up" we made little progress. We asked for help from Shanghai, recruited former military manufacturing companies to relocate from western China and tried to learn what other towns were doing. As a poor agricultural area, we felt we had no choice but to grow our local economy by attracting foreign direct investment (FDI). As a county, we were not authorized to recruit foreign investors directly, so we used our own funds to create a New Industrial Park and looked for opportunities to work with interested businesses. With few resources, one of the few things we could offer was service; so we did things quickly, efficiently and honored our agreements.

Kunshan 1950

Kunshan 1960

Kunshan 1970

On the left:
Kunshan1990

Shengtai New Farmers' Village

Q: What is the Kunshan Way?

A: It is about service; doing what needs to be done quickly and efficiently.

It's about being realistic; recognizing and using your advantages, which in our case was our proximity to Shanghai, our abundant land and labor, and overcoming your disadvantages, which for us was a lack of a developed industrial base.

It is about hard work; Kunshan's success would not have been possible without the dedicated work of its civil servants. They were always willing to do what was necessary when necessary.

It is about never being complacent; our rapid development created a foundation for attracting more businesses and industries that gave us a momentum advantage. But we have learned that anything we did yesterday must be improved if it is going to work tomorrow. In China, if you are not running as fast as you can, you are going to be passed by those who are.

It is about always looking outward for ideas and processes. A large part of our internal efforts were devoted to studying other economic development processes in places like Singapore, the Republic of Korea and Taiwan so we could adapt their ideas to our reality.

It is an ongoing process which is defined by the need to stay one half second ahead of our competitors so we can serve our people locally and nationally.

Q: Kunshan has an impressive track record. How has it been able to maintain its momentum as its leadership has changed?

A: combination of clear policy goals, higher government support, a willingness to

Looking at Huaqiao International Business District from Lüdi Road

learn, humility and a few successes have been the most important factors in creating and promoting the Kunshan Way. At its heart the Kunshan Way is a process which emphasizes the government's economic and social responsibility in ways which are fundamentally different from other models. The key to the Kunshan Way though is not the processes we use but the dedication of our people to our goals, our willingness to take risks, make mistakes and learn, from our experience and the experience of others.

We have had the benefit of clear consistent national policies which have emphasized economic development as a means to social progress. We have a committed leadership group who believe in and follow the system of service, innovative pragmatism and hard work which make up the Kunshan Way. While different leaders have adjusted their emphasis depending on the circumstances they found themselves in (promoting foreign/local business vs. cultural/urban development), their dedication, methods and drive have been the same. We have also benefited from the close attention paid to the selection of leaders by the authorities in Suzhou City and Jiangsu Province.

As we have learned, we have gained confidence. In the 1950s, China had a slogan "serve the people." A version of this, "be close to merchants," was later adopted by Singapore. When we started studying Singapore's economic model in the late 80's, we initially thought this meant "be close to capitalism," but they explained that this was simply an application of our original slogan which was meant to remind leaders that the quality of people's lives depended on the government's ability to promote economic development. It reaffirmed our commitment to the principles of "opening up," the idea that socialist goals and market mechanisms were not incompatible. It guided our development planning and service delivery.

We have a very strong commitment to training and education which involves every employee and Party member. In addition to our own Party school, we made full use of the Shanghai Pudong Cadre School branch in Kunshan and various national training programs. We also sent people to training courses in foreign countries like the US, Singapore and South Korea.

Q: Many bureaucracies suffer from "since I did nothing, I did nothing wrong" approach to their jobs. In Kunshan, "doing nothing" is not acceptable. How did this corporate culture evolve?

A: We tell people, "If you follow the principles of the Kunshan Way and you make a mistake, do not worry; professional mistakes will be forgiven, but personal mistakes will not" (it means literally that any mistakes in your personal life and dealings will end your career advancement). We believe that the best results are created when you lead by example. By having leaders who are willing to make and learn from their mistakes, we encourage those below to do the same. When leaders maintain high personal standards, they encourage others to follow.

We have had consistent support from the upper levels of government whose praise and attention gave us the confidence and energy to try harder. This can not be underestimated as an incentive when we were lucky enough to have high-level government leaders review and encourage your efforts—it energized us and helped us renew our dedication.

Q: Each generation comes to the realization that the best they can do is prepare others to lead. Do you have concerns about the future and the generations whose resolve has never been tested by hard times?

A: I am concerned about environmental issues in general and the spirit of public service in particular. The generations which created the PRC and lived through its first 40 years suffered hardships, but they willingly made sacrifices for the sake of creating a better future. Many of the urban children born after the mid to late 80s have not had to face the hardships their parents and grandparents confronted. I am concerned whether they will feel the same desire and/or dedication to "serving the people." While this is a concern which each generation has about the next, the rapid economic changes of the last 20 years have created an experiential divide whose effect is unknown. One of the areas I am interested in is the idea of service and volunteerism, which my granddaughter introduced to me after she returned from a trip to the US. I am hopeful that this type of idea can be taught to children in China from an early age and be something their parents can reinforce by example.

Q: The US media is often critical of China and many commentators accuse China of having a hidden agenda. What is China's agenda?

A: Our concern, locally and nationally, is how to improve the lives of our people. As far as we have come, we are less than halfway there. In addition to urban issues associated with our rapid development, we have 800 million people living in rural areas who are waiting for the scientific and sustainable society to mature.

For the last 30 years, we have used practical approaches, like the "white cat and black cat" perspective, to pursue our goals. While we are committed to our goals we have no map, so we used "crossing the river by feeling for stones" to find our way. The majority of the ideas and approaches we use have been learned from abroad and we are still in the process of "seeking truth from facts." So, while we have ideas about what works in Kunshan and China, we do not know what will work for others. While our economic success has attracted attention, our social goals are still on the horizon, so our struggle continues. The desire to create a better life for our people, now and in the future, is a shared goal of governments at all levels. But how it can be accomplished will differ depending on the situation and culture. Some may look at us as an example, but the only thing we can offer is some practical advice about the process we have gone through.

Q: Do you have any examples which would help people understand the Kunshan Way?

A: Yes, one of early joint ventures, in 1985, involving Shanghai No.1 TV Factory (Golden Star). The original agreement was that each side would contribute RMB 3

Going green—Using solar energy systems

million yuan to build a TV factory in Kunshan. Due to a number of reasons, Golden Star was unable to put up its share of the investment. It was decided that the project was too important to let go, so funds were borrowed. Golden Star ended up putting up 300,000 yuan and we put up 5.7 million. The factory was built and Golden Star sent a deputy factory manager and 20 retired workers to set up the factory and train the workers. Within two years, the factory had produced 200,000 TV sets, creating a net profit of 10 million yuan. As per the original agreement, Golden Star took a 3-million-yuan licensing fee and asked for 50 percent of the profits, leaving Kunshan with 3.5 million yuan.

No one was happy. The people in Kunshan asked why, after we put up the majority of the investment, Shanghai received the majority of the profit. The Shanghai people asked why such a profitable venture was built in Kunshan in the first place.

At a meeting to discuss and resolve the situation, I suggested the following:
To Kunshan: 400 local people (mostly farmers and students) were hired and trained to work in an electronic assembly operation which gave them valuable experience in a manufacturing area Kunshan hoped to grow; the city earned a 3.5-million-yuan profit which represented a 30-percent year-on-year return; the city collected over 3 million yuan in local taxes and 3 million yuan in salaries were paid, together with other benefits Kunshan received, the total exceeded 10 million yuan.

To Shanghai: I reminded them that Kunshan had provided the capital, land and labor to help build the factory at a time when they could not get the money.

The matter was resolved at the meeting, but more importantly it formed the basis of how Kunshan viewed its financial expectations when looking at economic development opportunities. We have since then always looked at the larger picture when evaluating opportunities.

Another factor which was critical to this example was our ability to keep our costs low: where other Economic Development Zones(EDZs) in China spent over 100 million yuan per square kilometer, Kunshan created its 3.75-square-kilometer New Industrial Park for a total cost of 12 million yuan. This allowed Kunshan to offer services and make deals which would be difficult for others to match.

Author's Note

At a time when many make disparaging remarks about politicians in general, it is a pleasure meeting someone with the kind of integrity and dedication which should be a model to others. If China had 100 such leaders working in economic development, it would be bad for the US. If he were in the US, he would be regarded as a national treasure.

Kunshan Municipal Government House

Strategy

Kunshan has a comprehensive "six transformations" strategy which is at the core of its current development direction.

Transformation 1: diversifying capital and ownership sources and markets.
Having relied mainly on FDI and exports to drive its economic development engine, Kunshan will concentrate on encouraging more domestic financing, control and market focus, to cut its exposure to international economic forces. Using its EDZs Kunshan is able to provide the expertise it has acquired helping foreign firms locate and develop in Kunshan. This recognizes and follows national priorities to cut risk from exclusively relying on foreign funded development and create a more balanced mix of international and domestic businesses and markets.

Transformation 2: moving from a primary and secondary, to secondary and tertiary economy.
Much of Kunshan initial growth was due to its ability to attract primary and secondary manufacturing industries; today Kunshan is moving its economic mix

towards secondary and tertiary manufacturing and a value added services economy. This means that Kunshan will be more selective about the industries and companies it recruits and supports. In some cases high labor, low tech, low value added, high environmental impact industries and companies will not be supported and may be encouraged to look elsewhere. This follows national directives to move China's economy to the next phase and allow it to compete internationally as well as nationally.

Transformation 3: Strategic clustering of industries and companies.
In the past, although Kunshan located industries and companies in its EDZs, it was not always according to an overall strategic master plan. Under the current administration and in response to the need to cut cost, conserve resources and encourage economic growth, Kunshan has been using cluster planning. The aim of this type of planning is to bring industries, supply chains, research facilities, educational institutions, high-quality livable environments and logistic support closer together in ways which cut resource usage, conserve energy and foster innovation, entrepreneurship and shorter concept to production cycles. This is one of the major transformations which will be key to Kunshan future growth. Unlike Western models where, despite zoning and land use plans, physical placement of the component pieces of the economic development puzzle are strewn about in an often Daedasque muddle, China's ability to plan and execute land use gives it an important competitive advantage. In China development cycles are dynamic and fast enough to allow non-disruptive movement of plants, infrastructure and people to create the desired synergies, an option which would not be available to its Western urban competitors. Again this follows national policy on economic development and resource conservation.

Transformation 4: from pyramid to olive.
Kunshan's rapid growth has resulted in a pyramid shaped social and economic structure, it is the Kunshan's and China's goal to change the shape of the society towards an olive structure, where a large prosperous middle class is the stabilizing factor in a harmonious society. By adopting economic policies which encourage balanced higher value added development including education, research initiatives and other human resource development Kunshan is positioning its human resources to compete in the global knowledge industries of the future. Backed by a supportive infrastructure they will be able to realize higher wages and profits from their endeavors. While many governments talk about their plans to leverage human resources and create a competitive and balanced society, few could match Kunshan focus and speed. Hundreds of millions of RMB are being dedicated yearly to this multi-pronged strategic mix of developing research facilities, attracting and supporting education institutions and recruiting human resources and industries. Unlike most governments, Kunshan has embarked on a pragmatic strategy to create the kind of society everyone talks about but few act on. Kunshan is following China's national priorities in this regard, but what sets it apart is the

Mr. Zhang Guohua, Kunshan Party Secretary

thoroughness and speed of its planning and implementation. Having interviewed the heads of the various economic and planning bureaus I was impressed by the logic, knowledge and attention to detail of these mostly under 40, internationally educated planners and administrators. They were able to explain every part of their strategic initiative from planning to review and implementation, something which is often missing in their Western counterparts.

Transformation 5: creating a sustainable high quality living environment.
Over the next 20 years Kunshan will continue its transformation from a mixed urban-rural to a high quality sustainable urban environment. Again this is a goal expressed by many and achieved by few. The difference is that Kunshan and China have the ability to control development in ways their Western counterparts can not. Like Transformation number 3, the clustering initiative, Kunshan can use its broad redevelopment tools and powers to physically transform their community.

For Kunshan creating a sustainable high quality living environment will be closely linked to the future of Shanghai. Its goals and plans are to offer its corporate culture and physical infrastructure as a convenient alternative to Shanghai. Key to this is creating the type of living environment which can attract and retain desirable segments of the community who can bring capital, ideas and jobs with them to Kunshan. Kunshan's completed 2020 and 2030 plans talk about how a mix of public amenities parks, transportation, hospitals, schools, economic opportunities and housing choices combined with their economic clustering strategy can create an ideal location for the headquarters of international and national companies. Given its track record, careful planning and the attitude of its business community, Kunshan looks poised to achieve its goal.

Unfortunately, while moving towards a sustainable high quality living environment is a national directive, few cities have the combination of natural advantages Kunshan has, abundant water resources, cultural attractions, transportation and proximity to Shanghai.

Transformation 6: balancing economic and social development.

China's rapid economic success has often outpaced its cultural, social and ecological growth. Kunshan and China's future, as reflected in its other transformation priorities, indicate a commitment to balancing economic priorities with cultural, social and ecological needs. Part of this effort is already underway: protecting and promoting its cultural heritage in its ancient water towns and Kunqu Opera; socially, it is implementing new medical, retirement and community programs for rural residents; ecologically, saying no to industries with high ecological impacts, building parks and public transportation. If you look at the pictures of Kunshan of even a few years ago and visit Kunshan today you will see and feel the scope of changes which have already been instituted.

To understand how cities in China, and Kunshan in particular, have been able to accomplish what they have over the last couple of decades you need to understand how cities are structured and work which includes not only the basics of government but the outlook and thinking of its leaders.

Party and Government

In the US, a city's economic development strategy depends on its elected leaders. The role of the elected leader's political party is limited to general policies and election issues. Once in office, the newly elected official uses a team of political appointees to create and implement economic and social strategies.

In China, since Party members comprise 90 percent of the government, separating the Party and the government is not a productive endeavor. The central Party leadership sets policy directives and the various localities are expected to implement them at the local level. Party positions are appointed by the next higher level of Party organizations, meaning the Party secretary and every other senior Party official of Kunshan are selected by the Party leaders in Suzhou.

Operationally, this system has allowed China to quickly close the gap between it and the developed world by creating a coordinated and focused effort. Unfortunately, very little is known outside China about the system. For the purpose of a general introduction and to simplify the discussion and the interview process, it was convenient to view the Party side as having a more direct role in strategy and the local government as having more day-to-day operational responsibility. In fact, there is no red-line separation.

Currently, Mr. Zhang Guohua is in his third year as Party secretary of Kunshan, prior to that he was mayor, for four years. The Party secretary of a city, because of the Party's oversight role, is generally viewed as the highest ranking official. What separates the role of a Party secretary from a mayor is as said before, very nuanced. At the city level, the Party, as an organization, is a smaller separate entity charged with policy, administration, training and oversight of Party members and the government as a whole. The mayor is in charge of the government which is the larger entity and includes all the operational bureaus which are responsible for day-to-day planning and operations. However, overlapping administrative and oversight responsibilities often blur the lines between the two.

Zhang Guohua's background is that he majored in biochemistry and subsequently had three years of training in international economic law.

Interview with Zhang Guohua

Q: What is the Kunshan Way?

A: For the last 20 years, Kunshan has been using a strategy which has four basic components: "opportunity from chaos," "enlarging the box to cover the solution," "inside the wall, outside the wall," and "Mashang Ban." Together, they are the major components of our strategic system.

Opportunity from Chaos

Kunshan is old; its early Stone Age settlements were the first

to start organized agricultural cultivation. Its people have learned to plant paddy rice more than 6,000 years ago and have developed the wisdom to see change as opportunity. As a farmer, you plant and tend every year, not knowing what the forces of nature or man will bring but knowing there is no other way. We use the same process for economic development; we invest and nurture industries and companies in hopes that they will provide jobs, better living standards and a sustainable local economy. Like farmers, we do not know what the future will bring, but doing nothing is not an option. Farmers choose the crops which will grow best and bring the most rewards; the government does the same with industries and companies. But, unlike farming where the seasons are dictated by the rotation of the Earth, economic development cycles are harder to predict. Kunshan's approach is to look for opportunities in times of change. When the economic winter comes, Kunshan starts planning for the spring which will follow, and when the spring comes we tend our industries and companies, giving them what they need to grow. In the fall we harvest and start preparing for the next season of change, knowing that winter will come again and the cycle will repeat.

Enlarging the Box to Cover the Solution

In the US, you stress "thinking outside the box" as a way of developing solutions to the dynamics of an ever-changing and competitive market. In China, our directives are national, "thinking outside the box" could be disruptive and confusing. Think hundreds of cities pursuing alternate ideas unrelated to the national priorities in a country the size and complexity of China: it would decimate the already difficult logistical task of coordinating planning and action. Kunshan's

On September 12, Groundbreaking celebration of InfoVision Optoelectronics's USD 3.3 billion, 8.5 generation LCD panel production line in Kunshan (China's most advanced)

answer has been to look at issues and develop solutions which fit within the box of national policies and directives. Again, the issue is perspective. In China, the emphasis is on coordinated policy and action. Whether you agree or not, it has been responsible for transforming the nation into a global economic force in the shortest time period to date. Working creatively within the system is a challenge, with its own issues, but it is what has set Kunshan apart. It is also one of the best examples of how cities in China are helping to power China's economic miracle by creating innovative approaches to national issues in ways that are constructive examples rather than confrontational distractions.

Inside the Wall, Outside the Wall

In the US and most other countries, economic development is more of a cheerleading exercise. By comparison, in China, it is a full-contact body sport. Kunshan has taken its strategy one step further than most cities in China, by supporting our industries and companies directly when it makes economic sense. Our concept is that, if you are part of a key industry, it is our responsibility to create the physical and business environment you need to prosper. This "we are all in the same boat" approach only stops at the factory wall where the companies are expected to do everything necessary to justify the support they're receiving. Whether it involves direct equity investment, investment incentives, recruitment subsidies, infrastructure support, fast decision making, logistics, economic matchmaking or building localized world-class supply chains, Kunshan will do what is necessary.

In Kunshan, we tend our industries and companies like diligent farmers, fertilizing and weeding as necessary. The concept of nurturing industries and companies gets a lot of lip service around the world but little meaningful action. Kunshan spends 5 percent of its annual budget just on building research and development facilities and recruiting human resources. It uses specialized vehicles, like EDZs, when necessary and its leaders will do their homework and learn about your needs before you have your first meeting. On the weeding side, Kunshan has become much more selective about which industries and companies it is interested in, i.e., low-tech, low-margin primary processing industries with large environmental impacts and need for water, and no need to apply or expect continued support.

"Mashang Ban"

"Mashang ban" translates to literally "do it now," and it is more than a slogan. Fast efficient service is part of our corporate government culture and, if you wish to test this, schedule a meeting with us and see what happens. Kunshan uses its size as an advantage, its staff and leaders are always available, always competitive. Our dedication to pushing the interests of our companies is well known, whether you area manager have to get an emergency order through the Export Processing Zone on a Sunday night at 3 or you arrive for a meeting at 12 midnight, Kunshan

Developing the future renewable energy research facility in Kunshan New and Hi-Tech Industrial Development Zone (KSND)

has and will continue to respond.

Q: Twenty years ago Kunshan was struggling. Today it is the No. 1 county-level city in China, how did this transformation occur?

A: There are many reasons which have to do with the realities of where we were and wanted to go.

We were realistic. We were a poor farming community with few industries and we knew that our future would be what we made it.

We recognized the advantages we had and used them. Being near Shanghai was an important factor, so were the years of experience we had inherited from being in the Yangtze River Delta trading area.

We focused on being creative and proactive. China is entering a new era, there was no road map. We received and studied the central government's policies and suggestions. But with limited resources, we felt we had to work harder and more creatively than the larger and more prosperous areas around us.

We looked for and took advantage of opportunities when we found them. When we heard about companies that were looking for locations we acted quickly. We did not wait for opportunities to come to us; we used our personal and professional networks to find business prospects.

We have been consistent in our thoughts and ideas; each generation of government leaders has worked on the same blueprint. Businesses were able to rely on consistent approaches which created a smooth collaboration between our bureaucracy and their administration.

Q: What drives Kunshan?

A: In a country which is so intensely competitive, we know our advantage is slim at best and whatever was done yesterday will not be enough for tomorrow. We started out very poor and we know we could be very poor again if we become complacent. To compete for business, we must be practical and service-oriented. Internally, we must be entrepreneurial, creative and dedicated to excellence. In all things, though we must anticipate, plan and follow through before others, we can not afford to be satisfied or to stop.

Q: Why is Kunshan government different from other cities? For instance, in many places, the motto seems to be "I did nothing so I did nothing wrong," and in Kunshan it's "Do it now"?

A: All cities in China follow the same central government policies and directives. Cities have different natural advantages and cultural strengths. We have been lucky that the combination of our advantages and our desire to improve has led to some success.

As said before, our people suffered greatly when they were poor and we are determined not to let them suffer again. Unlike a business, our goal is not about profits, it is about using economic progress to lift the lives of our citizens. To do this, we work collaboratively to identify and solve problems.

Q: Specifically what techniques do you use to motivate your colleagues?

A: All suggested approaches are discussed by the group. The assumption is: any suggestion has been carefully prepared and therefore must be carefully reviewed. No one person should make a decision unilaterally. The advantage is that, when you know your proposal will be discussed and reviewed by your leaders and co-workers, you will prepare your suggestions and plans carefully. This helps create a continuous quality loop which increases our productivity.

When there is a problem, it must be solved. Rather than asking our superiors "What should I do," we train ourselves to look at the problem and develop constructive suggestions which can then be brought forward for further consideration and refinement. In this way, we are able to get the best input from those closest to the situation and make decisions quickly.

We work as a disciplined team. We are a comparatively small unit of government and must support one another by working closely so that our actions will not have unintended adverse consequences, and so we are all clear about the goals and our strategies.

Q: Kunshan is often referred to as "Little Taipei" because of the large number of Taiwanese people and businesses here. It has obviously been a cornerstone of your success. Was this a conscious strategy?

A: The best way to answer this is to give you a short synopsis of the Kunshan Way (Kunshan's development history) which had four parts.

First, The 1980s was Kunshan's starting point; it was our first conscious attempt to change our economy, by shifting from basic agriculture to primary industries. To accomplish our goals we took advantage of the opportunities offered by the national opening-up policies, and when necessary, created our own development vehicles, like our industrial park, to attract investment. Many of the things we did, while directly in line with national policy, were different and required great courage to implement. Our central strategy was "connect to Shanghai on the east, cooperate with the military factories in the west, unify our villages and always look for new answers and approaches inside and outside of China", it served us well and was the start of our economic journey.

Second, after Mr. Deng Xiaoping's famous 1992 speech about the necessity of following the "opening-up" policy, we in Kunshan strived to follow the letter and the spirit of the policy. The Kunshan Way became about finding answers and implementing them. It marked the beginning of a thriving period for Kunshan which saw our focus shift from internal to external thinking. We seized the opportunities offered by Shanghai Pudong development and used KETD's listing as a national level EDZ to attract more FDI and forge strong co-operative ties to Taiwan. We created the infrastructure our industries and companies needed to be competitive. As we developed we started to see the need for increasing economic specialization in promising new areas like high tech and research which led to forming new EDZs.

Third, after the 1997 Asian financial crisis we had to quickly reassess and refocus our strategies. Our strongest economic partners from Taiwan were badly hurt by the crisis, but it also presented a whole new field of opportunities. We quickly changed our business strategy to "focus on Taiwanese, work with Japanese and Korean and try to attract European and American companies". To help our foreign enterprises we created new vehicles, like our Export Processing Zone, and increased our focusing on retention issues, like investment services and the environment. The strategy was a success and we were able to attract and retain more and more Taiwanese IT businesses. It also created an opportunity to integrate these businesses in ways which helped them be more competitive, by strengthening the supply chains these industries depend on.

Fourth, after the Sixteenth CPC National Congress in 2002 the Kunshan Way began another active transformation phase. Our new goal is to effect an economic change from low value added and tech to high value added and tech industries and companies as part of our overall goal of moving into the tertiary industrial and human resource industries. We are already considered as the demonstration area of a well-off society in Jiangsu Province, we are facilitating not only a more prosperous economy but also a better living environment and a harmonious and sustainable development society.

In terms of our success in attracting Taiwanese investments and businesses, it was due to the word of mouth advertising. Taiwanese businesses coming to the mainland were impressed with our service and told their friends. It helped that we also actively cultivated Taiwanese business associations. Today we have over 50,000 Taiwanese living in Kunshan. Not only have they brought their businesses but also wives, children, schools, hospitals and food. The clustering effect has been an effective tool for us, but initially it was about attracting jobs and industries.

Q: Kunshan's key industries are major exporters. How has Kunshan dealt with the financial crisis and what lessons have been learned?

A: To be honest, I was more than a little flustered by the financial crisis. Although I had had some previous experiences with global downturns it was clear that it was going to be a challenge of a different magnitude than I had experienced before. Fortunately, we had had some indications in early 2008 that something was coming and we took the opportunity to gather information from our industries, companies and government resources, it put us in a better situation to respond when the wave hit.

Kunshan has historically used periods of economic upheaval to look for the new opportunities and given the magnitude of the economic correction we wanted to make sure we were prepared. In the end we did a number of things to help our companies weather the storm, for instance we provided loans against receivables when the liquidity market dried up and prevented a number of unnecessary bankruptcies, and we aggressively focused on what we believe are new opportunities in the optoelectrical and outsourcing industries which are also supported by the central government.

The key to dealing with financial downturns for us has been to use it as an opportunity to increase capital investments in promising industries as others pull back, not only is it less expensive to buy and build but you are then ideally positioned when the market recovers. We have found it also very important to be prepared with quick counter measures. As a result in 2009, China's imports and exports decreased, but Kunshan's exports grew by 5.4% and our imports grew by

0.8%. Kunshan was very fortunate to be the only city at its level to have experienced positive growth during this period.

In some ways the financial crisis was good for us because it forced us to focus on our core strategies which has helped us become stronger.

Q: To get where it is today, Kunshan's leaders have consistently taken calculated risks, implementing innovative approaches to difficult issues. As a leading economic county-level city in China, will Kunshan concentrate on consolidating its gains or taking more calculated risks?

A: Based on what we have learned from watching other developing and developed countries, including Singapore and the US, we anticipate that the hard cost of doing business in Kunshan will rise as the economy develops. As this is not something we can control, our strategy is to concentrate on soft cost issues that we can. We see ourselves as responsible for planning and implementing economic development. The decisions we make about infrastructure, living environment, business recruitment are the keys to our economic future. To increase tertiary high value-added industries, we are aggressively recruiting entrepreneurs, scientists, technicians and managers in targeted industries, like LED, OLED and AMOLED display's, advanced injection molding, biotechnology component manufacturing, information technology outsourcing (ITO), business process outsourcing (BPO) and knowledge process outsourcing (KPO), new energy products, nano-metric materials, new agricultural products, food processing and entertainment and quality-of-life facilities like schools, hospitals, parks, sports facilities and teams.

At first glance, this list can appear disjointed but they are part of Kunshan's vision for an upscale community which attracts regional and world headquarters, international research facilities and world-class manufacturing. So the answer is yes, we will continue to take calculated risks to attract those opportunities which fire our vision as we do not feel that consolidating gains will allow us to be competitive.

Q: Can you be more specific about the strategies you intend to use to accomplish this?

A: We have a ten-point strategic plan:

First, build a modern three-part economic system based on high-tech products, advanced manufacturing capabilities, efficient supplier and logistic systems; sophisticated outsourcing services; state-of-the-art niche agricultural systems and products.

Second, cluster synergistic industries and companies with suppliers, research facilities and human resources to increase innovation, capacity, industrial integration and resource savings.

Third, develop a creative and competitive product and business development environment by subsidizing R&D and human resource recruitment in targeted high-tech industries like LED, OLED, RNA and advanced agricultural products and processes.

Fourth, strengthen our regional cooperation with Shanghai by identifying complementary products and services.

Fifth, develop a more integrated urban environment that utilizes rural areas to their highest and best use and puts in place needed infrastructure, public services and amenities

Sixth, Create a comprehensive education, medical services and social welfare system that covers all citizens and is part of a constant quality improvement system which assesses and improves the quality of life Kunshan has to offer.

Seventh, protect and promote our cultural heritage by finding ways of preserving and presenting it to both locals and outsiders, so people understand the cultural values and heritage Kunshan has contributed to China and the world...

Eighth, build a ecologically sustainable city which provides a high-quality living environment, including amenities which not only conserve resources but enhance life, by investing in infrastructure, sound urban planning and carefully guiding future economic development.

Ninth, continue to focus on creating an efficient and responsive public government structure which is able to recruit

The Taiwanese Commodities Exhibition and Trade Center

those who are dedicated to serving the people, obeying the rule of law, promoting the goals of a democratic system and who believe in the Kunshan Way.

Tenth, we will continue to train and attract those whose talents and wisdom can make our city economically more efficient, diverse and creative; socially more responsible; culturally more aware and politically more responsive to those we serve.

It has taken many hands to build Kunshan. Our future will continue to depend on the quality of our people and partnerships. To push ourselves, we set our goals high, look outward for ideas and remind ourselves that what we have accomplished in 20 years has depended upon being a half second ahead of our competitors.

Q: How do you maintain a balance between urban and rural needs?

A: Rural problems in China are complex. Rural development is one of my personal top priorities. Today we have the means to balance our society. Rising to the challenge of rural development is one of the primary directives from the central government.

Much of Kunshan's rural area will be eventually absorbed into city-town-village structures, as people migrate towards the larger metropolitan areas and agriculture becomes more mechanized. Our goal is to make sure we have a balanced approach to our rural and urban residents. Careful urban planning will be a key component of our approach. To date we have achieved one of the lowest differentials between urban and rural incomes in China, but we will continue to carefully focus on this issue so that we are able to create a balanced and sustainable society.

One of my regrets is that when I have gone abroad I have not had the time to visit areas outside the cities. In the future I would like to learn more about rural areas and how they are developing.

Q: Is it possible to promote Kunshan's model and experience?

A: China is huge and each place has a different situation. But a lot of the work is similar: urban-rural integration, industrial development, government service and promoting local competitive advantages. Kunshan is a small place, but our model may be meaningful in other areas. Each city in China has to work within the national policies and directives to create solutions. Our example is just one of many which can be studied and applied. If our approaches are seen as successful, maybe others will look at and adapt what is useful for their areas.

Author's Note

Pragmatic and self-effacing, I met the Party secretary in Beijing due to time constraints. He was polished, prepared and careful in his expression and manners. Rather than go on a great length about Kunshan's successes, he was much more interested in what needed to be done in the future. It was a refreshing change from some of the political fundraisers I have seen in the US where all you could hear was a litany of boasts and/or whining. On the other side, I wonder how much of Kunshan's success is due to the seemingly tireless efforts of its past and present leaders. He seemed well aware that to maintain their competitive edge they needed to work as hard today as they had in the past, but will future generations

of leaders have the same drive? The children born in the last 20 years have had great pressure but little physical hardship. Will they be willing to put aside their personal interests for the sake of the nation? The generations of Americans who were shaped by the Great Depression and two World Wars had different ideas about their nation than the generations that followed. One wonders how China's new generations will think.

Although he did not talk about it, I learned through other interviews that he played a decisive role in formatting a reaction to the current financial crisis. In April 2008 having seen unusual economic fluctuations of a number of key enterprises in Kunshan, he studied the market and developed the current strategic plan, which focuses on building an outsourcing industry, creating state-of-the-art research and development centers, strengthening the supply chains of key Kunshan industries by clustering companies and suppliers. His actions have kept Kunshan growing and healthy as other Chinese cities faced sharp declines. His approach to the issue was typical of the Kunshan Way, rather than worrying about the downside when he looked for the opportunities and seized them. His actions are now paying handsome dividends as China is quickly becoming a major outsourcing center and companies are flocking to Kunshan to take advantage of what it has to offer. I was particularly impressed with the fact that he actively reviews the economic performance of the companies in Kunshan, something which I wish Western political leaders were a little more cognizant of. It also brings to mind one of the defining differences between Eastern and Western city government systems, all Chinese officials are professional administrators while in the West anyone could be mayor if they are elected.

Huaqiao International Service Business Park

Operations of City Government

The mayor of a Chinese city, like a mayor in the US, is in charge of day-to-day government operation, which includes all city bureaus. Chinese cities have much more extensive planning, administrative and regulatory powers. Their ability to make direct investments in businesses, hold shares or even operate businesses dwarfs their US counterparts. The other edge of the sword is that they are more directly responsible for economic and social progress. The additional role of the mayor of Kunshan as director-general of Kunshan Economic and Technological Development Zone is an example of how directly connected his role is to creating economic results.

Mayors of Chinese cities have a comparatively larger and more extensive bureaucracy under them which attends to the day-to-day planning and operations of their cities. Following Mayor Guan Aiguo's interview, I have included interviews with some of the key individuals and departments which are useful to understand the operational side of Kunshan.

Guan Aiguo is mayor of Kunshan and concurrently director-general of Kunshan Economic and Technological Development Zone(KETD). He was born in Shandong. He majored in engineering (radio communications). He served formerly as the director-general of Suzhou's Science and Technology Bureau, Suzhou Intellectual Property Bureau, and Suzhou New & High-Tech Industrial Development Zone. He came to Kunshan in 2006.

Interview with Guan Aiguo

Q: How would you describe your personal experience in China over the last 50 years?

A: I was born in 1960. During my life, I have experienced three separate periods in China's modern history:

First, 1949 to 1966, a time when China was looking internally for answers to its development issues and had isolated itself from much of the world. Second, the "cultural revolution" (1966 to 1976), a time of chaos and suffering when China's industrial and educational operations came virtually to a halt. Third, the reform and opening up instituted under Deng Xiaoping (1978 to present), which has emphasized using education and knowledge from abroad to create a better society at home.

The sum of these experiences and our economic successes has convinced me that China is finally on the right path. We have strong ideological goals and pursue them with practical methods.

Q: How is Kunshan's success today related to China's history?

A: Kunshan's economic success is due to the courage and determination it has had to follow and implement China's national policies. The "spirit of innovation" has been important, but ideas without action are merely dreams. Kunshan is not a "dream"; it is a reality which is maintained with careful planning, intelligent people and hard work.

Although we are seen as successful today, in the chaos of the past we made many decisions which, while necessary at the time, wasted resources and had serious environmental consequences. The first step to learn from the past is to recognize and study what happened. In the future, as we implement our economic strategies and make decisions, we will look closely at the goals, use careful planning and measuring tools and rely on the knowledge and experience of our professionals.

Kunshan has a history of innovation. One of its famous ancestors was Mr. Zu Chongzhi. He was the leading mathematician of his time and was the first person to calculate the value of Pi (π), necessary to calculate the area of a circle, to seven digits, something that was only accomplished in the West a thousand years later. The spirit of Zu Chongzhi continues in Kunshan today. Like Zu Chongzhi, the lea-

Mr. Guan Aiguo, Mayor of Kunshan

ders of Kunshan continue to be very interested in not only the numbers but the ways numbers can be used to express useful and practical information.

Q: Most foreigners know little about China or its cities, other than Beijing and Shanghai. Unfortunately, the information available is often either general promotional materials, or information which, while useful to the central government, is not as useful to those looking to enter China's markets. Do you agree? How will Kunshan project its success to the rest of the world?

A: I agree. The first key is to be recognized by objective sources. For example, Kunshan was recognized by Forbes and the Taiwan Electrical and Electronic Manufacturers' Association (TEEMA). Forbes China ranked Kunshan as the No. 1 city in its category to do business in and No. 32 among all cities in China. TEEMA ranked Kunshan No. 1 in terms of comprehensive competitiveness for Taiwanese Electronics Companies looking to locate on the mainland of China.

The second key is to market our image in new ways that reflect our desire to be a center for innovative high-value-added industries. About five years ago, even before the financial crisis, we began planning our economic transformation. To give better expression to our new direction, we are asking companies to consider changing their "Made in Kunshan" labels to "Created in Kunshan." Although this may seem like a minor difference, it reflects where we are going, and when it is displayed on half of the world's laptops and a good percentage of other electronic equipment used everyday, we think it will have a major impact.

Q: What should people know about Kunshan's future direction?

A: In Kunshan, we believe that in the midst of chaos there are possibilities. As companies scramble to adjust to the post financial meltdown realities, new opportunities are emerging. Market emphasis is moving eastward and the pressure to find efficient ways to manufacture products and deliver services is greater than ever. As part of our socio-economic planning, we have chosen to focus on those industries which can be combined to create and maintain a harmonious and sustainable community. The industries we are interested in are:

First, advanced manufacturing industries including:

Electronics: Our focus is on creating the world's most all-inclusive and technologically advanced concentration of computer suppliers and manufacturers. By having a geographically concentrated comprehensive supply chain, manufacturers located in Kunshan will be able to improve communications, spark innovation and utilize efficient "just-in-time" delivery and processes, second to none. Because computer components are used in other consumer products, like cell phones, digital recorders, cameras, music players, etc., the supplier network will also be a draw

On the left:
Kunshan Pudong Software Park in Bacheng Township

to manufacturers of these other products and vice versa.

Precision manufacturing: We want to develop a precision machine manufacturing industry which can create auto parts, special vehicles, and injection molding.

Flat panel display: We will continue to focus on the development of TFT-LCD, OLED, AMOLED, PDP and other related upstream and downstream industries for the television, computer and portable electronics market as both a stand-alone industry and our-effort-to-support-our-electronics-industry.

New energy: We are interested in the production of solar energy and biomass energy products and creating a comprehensive upstream and downstream supplier network for both industries.

New materials: We will invest in and recruit companies and individuals involved with the research and production of new materials, new energy materials, biomedical materials and nano-metric materials.

Second, modern service businesses:

Kunshan will vigorously market itself as a prime regional/national headquarters to multinational corporations (MNC's) involved with logistics, banking, insurance, tourism, leisure, information technology, software development, consulting, and outsourcing.

We believe our combination of location, service, expertise, living environment and concentration on human resource development will be a winning combination in attracting headquarters operations not only for China but Asia as well.

Third, modern urban agriculture industries:

Our focus is on developing a seed industry, introducing new food and horticultural products for domestic consumption and export, processed food production and advanced agriculture R&D that support these sectors.

Fourth, modern urban soft power amenities:

Our plan is to create and attract sports facilities, local sport franchises, cultural attractions, hospitals, clinics, schools, universities, research institutions and training programs, which benefit our people and upgrade the local living environment.

Q: It is an extensive list, how does it all fit together?

A: Each area of economic development listed above is part of a comprehensive approach to Kunshan's future.

Our advanced manufacturing industry goals and efforts are split between supporting and enlarging our current computer and electronics infrastructure and developing the new technologies which will drive tomorrow's products.

Our modern service business strategy is based on our proximity to Shanghai, focused development, quality-of-life environment, developed infrastructure, excellent logistics, efficient government system and lower costs. We believe it will be attractive mix to companies, both foreign and domestic, who are looking to locate their China regional/national headquarters. The economic crisis has put China's domestic markets in a new light and we wish to capitalize on those companies who are coming to or expanding within China. The second part of this strategy is to attract and have available the type of support services which can support the scientific, technological and managerial enterprises we are looking to expand. Our desire to develop more soft power amenities is also aimed at improving the living environment.

Our modern urban agriculture efforts are aimed at helping our farmers climb the value-added ladder and turn out products which can be sold nationally and internationally. As an area with a strong agricultural heritage in the middle of one of China's major population centers, we wish to take advantage of our positioning and experience to introduce new agricultural products both as fresh and processed foods. Maintaining parts of the agricultural industry is also an important part of the quality of life we offer and a major difference between Kunshan and Shanghai.

Q: You have identified a list of goals and methods, which I am sure most cities, in China or the US, are also interested

Kunshan Software Park

in. What is the difference between your approach and the approaches you have seen in the US?

A: In the US, economic development is viewed as the main process for creating social benefits and harmony, while in China creating a harmonious and sustainable environment is our goal and economic development is just one tool we use to create it. We recognize that happiness based on consumerism is a moving target. The things we buy can not, in themselves, make us happy, but consumer activity and appetites can be harnessed to create an economy which provides jobs and higher standards of living for our people.

Q: In terms of attracting new and hi-tech industries to Kunshan, what beneficial policies and intellectual property (IP) protections do you offer? How is the market reacting to this?

A: I personally believe the issue is not about policies; policies are enacted by the central government and every city is charged with implementing them. The difference between Kunshan and other areas is how we use and implement the policies. Our success is due to our desire to understand what our industries and companies need to stay competitive. Subsidies and/or tax breaks will not, over the long run, create stable industries. If what a company or industry needs to be competitive is not available, it will fail or become a liability rather than an asset. In Kunshan, we build industries by clustering them in combinations which increase their overall chances of success. Robust supplier networks, efficient logistical access, reliable infrastructure, critical resource availability, fast and efficient processes, focused R&D and an institutional culture committed to understanding are what companies look for and need to be successful over the long run. We manage the stage and the companies are the actors. By understanding our role and theirs, both are able to concentrate on success. It is the basis of our "inside the wall, outside the wall" approach.

As regards the protection of intellectual property (IP), I was the first director-general of Suzhou Municipal Intellectual Property Protection Bureau, a bureau which I believed was crucial to the continued development of the knowledge-based economy we were looking to attract and grow. Our assumption was that IP protection was not about specific industries or projects, but the development of an efficient and transparent legal protection system. We developed the first Chinese urban IP trial court in Suzhou and later, the first county-level city IP trial court in Kunshan. Creating an efficient transparent process for dealing with IP issues rather than trying to solve each complaint as it comes in saves time and resources. The establishment of such a court demonstrates our true commitment to the issue. Like many innovations, the IP court was a new way of implementing national guidelines. It fostered continued rational economic growth. It is also a good example of how cities work within the system to "enlarge the box" when innovative solutions are needed.

I believe these types of approaches are crucial to the future of Kunshan and China. For Kunshan to implement its strategy of climbing the value-added ladder into tertiary industries and knowledge-based development, we need to be able to give people and companies assurance that their research efforts will be protected.

So, in addition to the IP court, we provide legal protection and financial support to inventors who want to register their patents and copyrights. Again, this is a policy we developed. Each year, we spend 5 percent of our total city budget supporting R&D and recruitment; 4 percent on R&D; and 1 percent on recruitment. One and half a billion yuan has been spent over the past three years developing research facilities and recruiting needed technical and professional staff. Since 1999, we have attracted seven colleges to come to Kunshan, which put us No. 1

The planned Industrial Technology Institute

in this regard. In addition, we continue to work closely with Tsinghua University on the joint research park and industrial partnerships. We are also expanding our international educational programs. For example, we have finalized an agreement which will bring a satellite campus from Duke University to Kunshan next year.

Author's Note

Different Perspectives

It is worth noting that the mayor of Kunshan emphasized several times during the interview that the city's economic efforts are a means of improving the living conditions and lessening the economic disparities, between urban and rural residents. Chinese county-level cities include both urban and rural areas. By US standards, they are, in fact, a district form of government. Having mixed constituencies complicates goals and administration in ways US city leaders do not have to contend with.

Message

As mayor, he plays a key role in delivering Kunshan's "message." Internally, he shares the responsibility of maintaining Kunshan's corporate culture, for instance, customer service delivery (Mashang Ban), creating expectations and measuring progress. Externally, he is in charge of the team effort which carries out Kunshan's focused economic development strategy, recruiting desirable companies and industries, making sure the service delivery process and mechanisms are working properly.

Looking Outward

Having traveled abroad extensively, Mayor Guan Aiguo has taken every opportunity to study existing development models in other countries, like Singapore and the Republic of Korea, and then adapt them for China. On a side note, he made a point of expressing his fondness for Harley Davidson motorcycles and has even visited their Milwaukee production facility. It illustrates a difference in how city leaders in China and the US see themselves and the experiences and influences they see as impor-

tant. I have rarely heard a US mayor talk about the importance of learning new development approaches from other countries.

Planning

Area planning, both rural and urban, a crucial part of the government's efforts, is an important part of his responsibilities. Kunshan's future has to be carefully managed because of its high-value-added potential and its ecologically sensitive location in the Yangtze River Delta. To tap its potential, Kunshan has to create and maintain a high-quality living environment.

The mayor also has direct responsibility to make sure the mechanics of doing business in Kunshan are operating effectively and efficiently. Because city government plays such an important role in business—this is the frontline of Kunshan's efforts.

Innovation

Kunshan's leaders view innovation and business development as a joint venture between government and business. The new generation of leaders are taking increasingly more sophisticated steps to foster new approaches. Intellectual property courts, subsidized patent filings, R&D facilities, direct equity investments, economic matchmaking and international human resources recruitment are just a few of the things which Kunshan does routinely. It definitely crosses the line which we in the US see as separating government from business. But it is difficult to argue with the results.

The interview was a pragmatic glimpse into how a mayor in China sees his role. Rather than a passive "let's hope things happen" approach, Kunshan has a plan, strategies and the will and experience to put their plan into action. This is the side of China that few people see, the part which explains how China has moved forward so quickly. So, if you come to Kunshan and want to talk about bringing a business which fits Kunshan's vision, or you just want to show off your Harley, you should schedule a meeting with Mayor Guan Aiguo.

Interview with Ms. Hang Ying

Hang Ying, Director of Publicity Department of Kunshan City Party Committee

The Publicity Department in a Chinese city plays a vital information role which cuts across all departments and levels of government. In addition to coordinating the message, they also enforce it. Government and Party officials are graded on their ability to clearly express the city's message. It is always a good place to visit as they can be a gold mine of information about who to contact in different departments about specific issues. While this is not necessary in Kunshan, because of their case-manager system, if you're looking at different cities in China they can be a valuable resource.

Ms. Hang Ying, Standing Committee Member of Kunshan City Party Committee, Director of Publicity Department of Kunshan City Party Committee

Q: What is the Kunshan message?

A: Kunshan's economic success story often obscures the part its people play in creating it. Lost among the numbers is the fact that it is Kunshan's people who have been shaping the city's character and direction. Our people are proud to be part of Kunshan and it is their support which has been the vital ingredient in making it successful. We have been fortunate to have strong visionary leaders who lead by example. But they work to serve the people and it is the pride which we see in our people that drives us to work hard and do more.

For example, when a businessman was scouting Kunshan as a possible location, he visited a hospital and, while looking around, struck up a conversation with someone standing in line. The Kunshan native asked if he was local and when the gentleman explained what he was doing, the man told him that in that case he could go to the front of the line, because everyone would willingly pass their turnup if he was willing to bring jobs to the area. The man subsequently located a business in Kunshan.

This spirit of embracing opportunity and responsibility has a long tradition in Kunshan. Philosopher and Kunshan native Gu Yanwu said, "Everybody is responsible for the fate of his country" at the end of the Ming Dynasty. It was a radical and innovative idea given the feudal times, but it established a feeling of shared responsibility which has persevered to this day. It is evident in the sacrifices our people have made and the courage they have had to continually try new approaches and ideas. Beyond just our local interests, we hope that things that worked for us can be used by others in their planning process. It is our way we can honor our ancestors and pass the wisdom to our children.

Q: You seem to be emphasizing the social issues more than the economic accomplishments, why?

A: To me, the cultural and economic progress in Kunshan are like two sides of a folding fan, one without the other would be unbalanced and incomplete. Part of our job is to let people know what the future holds and we always stress that culture and economics must be balanced to make a complete picture. Ultimately, our character is our true strength and, as we go forward with the next phase of our economic plan, it will become even more important. To attract and retain the best and brightest, we must show them why living and being part of Kunshan is special. Tall buildings and fast trains do not by themselves create a community. We believe that, once people know and understand the things which are part of the Kunshan Spirit, our respect for our traditions, foods, customs, ancient buildings, natural landscapes and culture, they will feel something they want to be part of.

Q: How would you sum up the Kunshan Spirit?

A: In 2007, Kunshan city government organized an effort to identify the words which expressed the spirit of Kunshan using a survey of local people, the result was "open, comprehensive, creative and excellent." Everywhere you go in Kunshan, you will see people who believe that tomorrow will be better than today, and this is the true reward for our efforts.

Author's Note

I was pleasantly surprised by Ms. Hang's reaction to my questions, rather than give stock answers about the economic accomplishments of her leaders, she spent her time talking about the people of Kunshan and how special they feel about their city and accomplishments. It is unfortunate that more people in her position do not do the same. I agree with her assessment that this will be the rare pearl which enchants the eye and holds the heart.

Kunshan New Culture and Art Center (underway), investing in culture old and new

Multiple Vice Mayors

Every city has multiple vice-mayors who function like cabinet ministers, each has a portfolio of responsibilities which they are directly responsible for. Because Chinese city governments are larger and more directly involved in the life and prosperity of their cities, it would be difficult for one person to oversee all of the activities.

Vice Mayor Huang Jian of Kunshan is responsible for science & technology; international trade & cooperation; the Foreign Affairs Office; the Taiwan Affairs Office; overseas Chinese affairs; tourism; industrial & commercial activities; quality supervision, food and drug supervision, customs inspection and quarantine; and exporting issues and support.

I had the pleasure of sharing a hearty Kunshan brunch of Ao Zao Mien—Kunshan smoked fish, fresh water shrimp, Qiandeng lamb, three-flavor meatballs and Zoushi Duck—with the vice mayor at the Aozao noodles restaurant near Tinglin Park. We sat in the private state dining room used by central and provincial government leaders who visit Kunshan. As the locals say, you can not say you have gone to Kunshan unless you have tasted some of its famous delicacies. Evidently, this is true because the guest book bore the inscriptions of some of China's most famous leaders. Unlike most state dining rooms, the dining room looked out across the stairwell to the large second-floor dining room which made it a pleasant and jovial spot to enjoy an outstanding meal. Vice Mayor Huang was waiting for us and was passing the time watching the results of the Taiwanese election. It is notable that the people of Kunshan are news junkies: whether in a cab or in a meeting room people seem to be either looking at newspapers or listening to financial reports.

Interview with Huang Jian

Q: What are the key elements of Kunshan's approach to economic development?

Tinglin Road today

Mr. Huang Jian, Vice Mayor of Kunshan

A: There are four parts to our success: We have a comprehensive local business and social culture; we provide excellent government's service; we concentrate on learning how to fish rather than asking for one; and we divide by industries, not nationalities, which means we are color-blind when it comes to opportunities. The only issue is how to create a win-win situation for all sides.

Q: What are your economic development priorities?

A: Our top priorities are supporting existing and bringing in new businesses. Currently our major industries are electronics (over 60 percent of the local GDP) and mechanical manufacturing. We intend to support our existing industries by using vertical integration strategies which support efficient development and production. To accomplish this, we will continue to strengthen current industrial development and supplier chains by recruiting strategic companies and industries to Kunshan. New business areas we intend to pursue include: optical display technology (TFT, LCD & OLED), renewable energy, biotech RNA production, new materials (carbon fiber and nano-materials), and environment-friendly equipment manufacture (including design, component manufacturing and assembly).

Q: What is your implementation plan?

We have a 1 + 3 + 10 strategy.

One: Research:

For example we are building a new Industrial Technology Research Institute which will be devoted to developing new and add-on technologies for panel displays, RNA production, industrial robotics, industrial and commercial sensors and network technology. We see research as the engine which will power the next phase of our economic development, we are committed we are using our own funds to build the research institute.

Three: Three development zones:

KETD: It is a national-level development zone which will take a lead role in developing our optical display industries by targeting companies that have promising intellectual property and creating supportive supply and development chains, so companies located in Kunshan will have a competitive advantage.

KSND: It is currently a provincial-level development zone (will be upgraded next year to a national-level development zone). It will continue to pursue companies with promising intellectual property and advanced manufacturing capabilities which support targeted industries.

Tsinghua Science and Technology Park

Huaqiao: Currently a provincial-level development zone, it will try to attract leading international and domestic companies to locate their China and Asia headquarters in Kunshan. They will use the fact that while we are next to Shanghai we can offer a higher level of services without the costs and bureaucracy. We will support this effort with the continued development of advanced logistics and outsourcing services. Our competitive advantage is a mixture of low political risk, direct access to China's market, excellent proactive business support, favorable location and an attractive living environment. We believe this is a competitive combination which will be attractive to companies who are looking for a strategic headquarters location for China and Asia.

Ten: Ten national specialized industrial initiatives:

We are concentrating on ten industrial initiatives, split into five current and five future ones. The current five are: software development, industrial molding, sensor technology, renewable energy and integrated circuits. The future five are: equipment manufacturing, RNA biotech, robotics, sports and leisure products, and infant and children's products. For example, we are currently building the world's leading infant and children's products R&D facility in conjunction with Goodbaby, which is the world's leading player in the market. We believe by limiting our areas of interest to related tertiary industries we can create successful cluster environments. We believe our cluster approach will also create intellectual and technical expertise that can enhance the competitive position of companies located in Kunshan.

Q: There are some large OEM companies in Kunshan. They are powerful business promoters but extremely cost sensitive. What is Kunshan's strategy to retain these industries if cost pressure increases?

A: In the past, we advanced our development by using cheap land, inexpensive labor, financial incentives and efficient service delivery. The companies we attracted were those most sensitive to these issues. As time has gone by, the competition from other areas, in and outside China, has become fiercer. To stay competitive, we have altered our efforts. Rather than trying to compete on individual issues, we concentrate on creating a more competitive overall business and living environment. The elements of this approach are:

Fast efficient service (one-stop administration center and Mashang Ban which has even surprised me with its effect). China has a strong government system which requires foreign businesses to work closely with the local authorities. To overcome the concerns of our foreign business clients, we constantly strive to have the most efficient and client-oriented service systems. It gives us a strong initial competitive advantage as new businesses entering the area are always extremely concerned about legal issues, communications, schedules and costs.

We are constantly improving our integrated industrial supply chain support system. By clustering suppliers and clients, we are able to create a positive investment and innovation spiral. Having your main suppliers and customers across the street creates an efficient and responsive system which allows companies to concentrate on their core competencies and frees up time and resources for further research and development.

We cooperate closely with Shanghai on transportation, financial and human resource issues. By integrating our logistics efforts with Shanghai, we are able to improve our capabilities, which is vital to companies that are dealing with China's immature distribution systems and channels. Having a selection of the world's largest and most sophisticated financial firms 18 minutes away gives our business access to the services they need and are familiar with. As most people are not familiar with Kunshan, our proximity to Shanghai is a major factor in attracting human resources. The fact that we

can offer a great lifestyle at less cost with all the advantages of Shanghai is a major draw.

Q: It sounds like a fairly comprehensive plan. When was it developed?

A: Kunshan has been thinking about transforming its economic structure since 2002, much earlier than central government's emphasis and guidance. In looking ahead, for the reasons stated above, we saw the need for new development engines. We felt that to stay competitive we needed to move our economy from "investment and export" to a more balanced economic base which relied on new product and technology development for both the export and the domestic market. In essence, we decided we needed to shift from primary & secondary industries to tertiary industries. At the same time, we realized that, to accomplish this, we would have to capitalize on our existing manufacturing base and help propel them from OEM's to ODM's and branded companies.

Q: How do you plan to accomplish this?

A: We have a five-part transformation strategy which will involve:
Changing the focus of our economic development efforts from resource-dependant to sustainable and green industries. In the past, we accepted businesses which had ecological side effects. We no longer have an open door policy for these types of industries and companies. This is an important part of our efforts to create a better living and working environment attractive to corporate headquarters and high-level human resource recruitment.

We will continue to use our business development vehicles, like our EDZs, to target and attract industries. To give them the tools to compete, we will pay special attention to both physical infrastructure and human resource issues, which we see as the "hardware and software" of our development model. As part of this effort, we will continue to work on and improve our service delivery systems which will require increased technical and professional knowledge. Our goal is to actively pursue opportunities rather than wait. To do this effectively, we have to combine service and knowledge.

We will drive development using our research and development facilities which will be tasked with creating the next-generation solutions and products for our industrial base.

Exports will continue to be a vital part of our economy. To support and expand this area, we will continue to improve physical logistics, supplier and customer clustering, attract technical and professional talents and help our industries move from OEM's to branded producers.

Continuing to upgrade our business and living environment. A suitable environment is vital to our strategy to attract talented innovators, technical professionals and investors. To accomplish this, we will be upgrading living conditions by encouraging development of higher-end apartments, better schools, improved medical facilities and more community assets, like parks, leisure venues and tourist attractions.

Q: What is Kunshan's role in China and its relationship with the central government?

A: Kunshan has played host to many of the most important leaders over the years. We were fortunate to get praise for our efforts and to have been referred to as a successful representative of the "opening-up." Many former leaders from Kunshan have been promoted to higher positions in other areas. We are very proud and confident of our people, strategies, efforts and accomplishments. But we are aware that yesterday's achievements do not create tomorrow's. We know that if we want to continue to be successful we need to work even harder and smarter than we have in the past. In terms of our role in China, we are just one city; and like all other cities in China, we trust and follow the central policies, which have guided China's economic "opening up."

Q: Given what Kunshan has done for business, can it do the same for other areas like soccer?

A: I always talk to foreign guests about our cultural offerings and how we can combine the best of Kunshan's traditional culture and Western ideas. I would welcome the opportunity to having a soccer team or other sport teams in Kunshan as urban name card and to show what the Kunshan Way could do for sports.

Author's Note

The last question was tongue-in-cheek as many in China are disappointed with its soccer program, which, given the amount of national interest and size of the population, should be at a higher level than it currently is.

EDZs, the Building Blocks of Success

Kunshan's EDZs are its economic building blocks. Each EDZ is a separate entity licensed by either the central or provincial government. Each has its own director and staff. They report to Kunshan's government as well as to the bodies which license them. To give you a sense of what they are, what they do and what they have to offer, we interviewed relevant leader of each EDZ.

EDZs in China have followed models developed in other parts of Asia, like the Republic of Korea and Singapore. Although we have EDZs in the US, they do not really compare. EDZs in China, like cities, are entities which work on the local level to accomplish national priorities. Many of China's EDZs have been marvelously successful but many more have failed. At their best, EDZs are focused business incubators and developers which go proactively after business. They tend to focus on discrete areas as they grow.

There are four development zones in Kunshan: the Kunshan Economic and Technological Development Zone (KETD), the Huaqiao International Service Business Park, the Kunshan New and Hi-Tech Industrial Development Zone (KSND) and the

The Times Mansion, a modern office complex in the KETD

Kunshan Tourism and Holiday Zone. They form the cornerstones in Kunshan's economic development engine.

The KETD is an international standard EDZ. It has a mature administration and offers a number of favorable tax and investment policies. It has three main industries: IT, Precision Instruments and Daily Sundries. It also has a number of sub-zones which include the Export Processing Zone, Free Trade Zone, Optoelectrical Park and Business Incubator for Overseas Chinese Students. The KETD has ranked as one of the top four national EDZs for seven consecutive years by MOFCOM. In 2009, the KETD total exports were the largest of any EDZ in China.

The Huaqiao International Service Business Park is the only provincial-level EDZ focusing on business development. It has four main focuses, being a national and international Business Processing Outsourcing (BPO) center for companies interested in hedging their political risk and entering the China market; a cross-straits commercial cooperation center, which provides centralized procurement, wholesale, retail and exhibition services aimed at introducing Taiwanese products to the mainland; an attractive headquarters location for international and domestic companies looking for a regional or Asia presence, with all the amenities of Shanghai without the cost and bureaucracy; and as a satellite commercial park for those looking for strategic locations on the outskirts of Shanghai.

The KSND is a national-level high-tech development zone, whose roles include being a new development zone for innovation and as a demonstration zone for low-carbon development. The main function of the KSND is to promote the transformation of technological advancements into high-tech products. Its main industries include precision instruments, industrial molding, renewable energy (solar and wind), OLED display, CNC's and robotics, and biomedical industries like the production of ribonucleic acid.

The Kunshan Tourism and Holiday Zone occupies a total planned area of 29.88 square kilometers and has two comprehensive resort areas, Yangcheng and Dianshan lakes. Kunshan's tourism comprises three parts: waterside towns, leisure style resorts and urban sightseeing. There are five AAA national scenic areas and ten tourism demonstration areas. In 2010, nine refined tourist routes have been developed for those visiting the 2010 Shanghai World Expo who want to take some time to experience Kunshan.

Interview with Lu Zongyuan

Lu Zongyuan, Vice Secretary, KETD Party Working Committee,
Vice Director, KETD Administrative Committee
The KETD has consistently broken new ground in every aspect of economic development. If you believe excellence is about what you do, there is no question that

the methods and approaches the KETD has pioneered should be required reading for anyone seriously interested in economic development models. It is difficult to adequately express how impressed I was with the KETD's accomplishments. It is certainly a great reflection on those who were involved.

Q: The KETD has continued its success even during the financial crisis, what do you attribute this to?

A: Over the years, China has developed three areas of competitive strength. Nationally, our competitive strengths come from the legal system and economic development policies we have developed. Regionally, our competitive strengths come from the investment environment we have created. At the local level, we believe that KETD's support model creates a competitive advantage to those corporations within our EDZs. Under this scenario, KETD's role is to amplify the competitive advantages of its companies so that on a head-to-head basis being located in Kunshan becomes a critical competitive issue. In 2009, our local economy grew by 15 percent, which shows that the three-tier support system is working.

Q: To what do you attribute Kunshan's success and what sets KETD apart from EDZs in other cities?

A: I believe that our value added is the speed and efficiency of our service. Companies who come to Kunshan need to get up and run as quickly as possible. By simplifying and speeding up the process, we allow companies to concentrate on competing for business rather than wasting time and resources. I also believe that our favorable location (close to Shanghai), cultural traditions, pleasant climate,

Gateway to and from the Export Processing Zone of KETD

educated workforce and talented people are contributing factors to our success.

Q: How has the KETD evolved?

A: The history of the KETD and that of Kunshan are intertwined. Over the last 30 years, it has undergone four transformation periods.

(1) From agriculture to industry. In the 1980's, a few township industrial enterprises were established. The major event was the creation of the New Industrial Park (3.75 square kilometers, base of today's KETD) in 1985. To attract investment, we felt we needed a vehicle which could attract and cater to the enterprises. Unfortunately, as a township, we were not eligible for national, provincial or local financial support. Our solution was to fund the park ourselves.

(2) From internal to external. During the planned economy period, very few SOEs(state-owned enterprises) built factories in Kunshan. Without an established domestic industrial base, Kunshan decided to look outside for foreign capital for its development. The KETD played a leading role in this effort by creating and offering economic tools and incentives that fit the needs of the businesses we wanted to attract. In 1992, the park was finally approved by the central government as a national KETD. Importantly, unlike other 14 open coastal cities with national-level EDZs, the KETD was developed and paid for by Kunshan. Because we used our own money, we paid very close attention to the costs and were able to create an efficient cost-effective park that still had the infrastructure to support our businesses. It gave us a competitive advantage in terms of the deals we could make.

By the 1990s, we were successfully attracting large amounts of foreign capital from Hong Kong, Taiwan and other places around the world. But the companies coming in were mainly labor-intensive and low-added-value OEM manufacturers. In early 1990s, we identified an opportunity as increasing costs, competition and other market pressures started causing a shift in the Taiwan-based manufacturing industry. We successfully started recruiting businesses looking for better economic conditions. Unfortunately, it was difficult and expensive for Taiwanese companies to comply with the import/

export restrictions which were in place. To deal with the problem, we looked at Taiwan Hsinchu Science and Technology Industrial Park model for creating a duty-free import/export zone which would allow companies to import, add more value and export without having to pay taxes or be subject to import/export regulations and currency controls. After studying the Hsinchu model, we applied to create the Central Export Processing Zone. In 2000, it was approved by the central government as the first duty-free import/export zone in the country. Since then, 55 Chinese cities have opened similar zones. The Central Export Processing Zone allowed us to attract major laptops, cameras and projector manufacturers. Currently, about 50 percent of laptops (over 60 million sets) and 15 percent of digital cameras (about 15 million sets) are made in Kunshan. In 2009, the Central Export Processing Zone contributed 41.8 billion dollars import & export volume, as well as RMB 223.2 billion output value.

(3) From diversified to concentrated. The success of the Central Export Processing Zone also helped us create strong locally based industrial supplier chains, as our new large manufacturers brought in and attracted components makers. From this, we began to understand the meaning and importance of industrial chains and vertical integration. Since then, IT has become our main industry, accounting for about 50 percent of our local GDP. However, the majority of it is low-margin business that relies more on economies of scale than innovation. Although we control the mass production and even designs, the value added is limited. Large brands like Toshiba, HP and Dell control the high-value-added processes, such as R&D, branding, sales distribution and components acquisition. As we became more knowledgeable about the industries, we realized that we could easily lose these industries if unfavorable market forces moved against us.

(4) From low end to high end (the future). As we move forward into the next phase, we are encouraging companies to develop their own service/products, brands, marketing and distribution. To do this, we support R&D by building facilities, directly subsidize IP filings and defense, provide human resource recruitment incentives and give introductions to China's domestic markets. By doing this, we hope to shift our main industry focus from secondary to tertiary industries. We are also actively recruiting the types of services and

building a living environment which is attractive to innovative knowledge-based enterprises.

Q: What is your personal understanding of differences between the economic theories and models used in the East and West?

A: There were three essential truths about change in the book of *I-Ching* (or *The Book of Changes*, an ancient Chinese philosophy text which explained and predicted the natural and human conditions and interaction) that I believe apply to economic development:

Complex changes: The changes which are hard and sometimes impossible to predict; they are the normal ups and downs which depend on complex factors.

Simple changes: Changes which, like the seasons, occur regularly and predictably.

Things that do not change: Activities and cycles which never change like the human nature and economic cycles.

In the West, my sense is people think they can predict and control change, while in the East we believe that change is a constant and a variable, simple and complex, and that it is up to individuals to maintain their direction by understanding and using the nature of change to look for opportunities. It is why we in Kunshan welcome rather than fear change, because we feel that, if we study carefully and act swiftly, we can continue to find opportunities.

Author's Note

It is refreshing to meet people like Mr. Lu Zongyuan. He is intelligent, direct and dedicated both to his role in the KETD and the government. He is one of a number of people I met in Kunshan who made it apparent why the city is first in its class. Meeting him and understanding what the KETD has done and is doing should be a requirement for those wishing to master how to use economic development vehicles to create change. Rather than whining about the circumstances he and his team create the solutions they need to move forward, a skill set you rarely see.

Interview with Tang Naixin

Tang Naixin, Deputy Director, the Administration Committee of Huaqiao Economic Development Zone, and former Secretary-General of Kunshan City Government

Q: I interviewed a number of businesses who have located in Huaqiao and they consistently rave about the speed and quality of service they receive. Is this the main theme of your business model or are there other things potential businesses should be aware of?

A: Kunshan's success is based on constant forward thinking and structural transformation. The sense of service, which is ingrained in Kunshan's culture, has been constantly improved as part of our economic development strategy. In the 1990s, we offered honesty, enthusiasm, location, low costs and favorable economic development incentives. In 2000, we started upgrading our services to match the needs of the new industries we were trying to bring in. The development center created a one-stop shopping service center for companies and our one-point-contact project management system made sure things went smoothly. We also put more emphasis on how to use strategic planning to create win-win situations. In 2006, we finished our development plan to use the Huaqiao EDZ as a bridgehead into the human resource and logistics industries. Our targets were human resource firms who were looking for back-office support locations. The idea for developing this type of business came from McKinsey and Co. At that time, financial service and BPO (business process outsourcing) were quite unfamiliar to us. However, based on the seminars we attended in Beijing, Shanghai and Hong Kong, as well as McKinsey's recommendation, we developed our ideas and master plan. At present, we are very proud to be the leading city of BPO business in China.

Promoting business—Huaqiao International Business District

Q: What services do you provide?

Creating a setting—Huaqiao International Business District's Central Park

A: Since all Chinese cities have similar slogans and the same policies, the difference is the quality of service. To be successful, we believe we need to have an in-depth knowledge of our clients' industries and needs.

The more we learned about the needs of our customers the more we became convinced that service and environment are the most powerful incentives to attract our target businesses. In terms of environment, we have carefully included all the necessities of business and quality-of-life amenities that our clients said were factors in their location decisions. In terms of transportation, we are minutes away from the Hongqiao Airport, across the street from the Shanghai subway line. We have a master-planned office park which includes offices, hotels, conference facilities, and a 400-million-yuan training center. In terms of living, the park has multiple types of housing, grocery stores, retail shops, schools and an 800-million-yuan sports and entertainment facility.

Q: Why would companies locate in Huaqiao?

A: We offer political stability and entrance to China's market in a unique location which has access to Shanghai without the cost and traffic congestion. Based on our focus groups and other market research, our goal is to make people who come to Huaqiao feel like they are still in Shanghai. We believe that, over the next few years, there will be a major move by back-office operations to diversify their locations and we are ready for them. It is our belief that the best is yet to come and, with creative thinking and fast service, we can seize the opportunity.

Author's Note

I interviewed Deputy Director Tang Naixin at the Hilton Double Tree Hotel located in the EDZ. From the hotel entrance, I could see Shanghai across the street. I toured the new training center and talked to businesses that had located in the numerous new skyscrapers which dot the park. While the area still had the raw feeling that new concrete creates, I could not help but be impressed by Kunshan's willingness to go after a market that is still evolving in China. Once again, their timing seems to have been impeccable as the number of new businesses moving in attests.

Interview with Rosemary Tao

Rosemary Tao, Deputy Director, Kunshan New and Hi-Tech Industrial Development Zone Administration Committee

KSND is the Kunshan New and Hi-Tech Industrial Development Zone. Rosemary had just come back from a graduate study program at the University of Maryland, one of over 20 officials sent by the Suzhou municipal government.

Q: What are the highlights of KSND's development?

A: KSND was established and approved by the China Ministry of Science & Technology as a hi-tech industrial park in 1994. In April 2006, KSND was approved by the Jiangsu provincial government and the National Development and Reform Commission as a provincial-level new & hi-tech industrial development zone, with the following missions:
- To develop manufacturing, trade & service industries as part of China's 11th Five-year Plan period;
- To develop the following six industries: IT, OLED, new materials, renewable energy, industrial mould manufac-

turing, modern trade, and service industry;
- To build up a high-density new & hi-tech industry development zone;
- To be one of the most competitive new & hi-tech industrial zones in China.

Q: What progress have you made on these goals?

A: After 10 years of development, KSND has attracted more than 600 foreign-invested projects from all over the world. The total investment has reached 8 billion US dollars, with the utilized capital exceeding 4 billion US dollars ("utilized capital" refers to the capital actually invested as opposed to capital which is committed).

KSND covers a planned area of almost 52 square kilometers, including three different sections:

Section A is located at the north region of Kunshan City. It is already concentrating on the industrial mould industry; it is also the site of Kunshan's Science & Technology Incubator Service Center which focuses on R&D services for the trade and service industries.

Section B is situated south of Kunshan City, it focuses on six new & hi-tech industries: IT (automotive electronics); new types of energy (solar energy); industrial mould manufacturing; logistics; new types of materials (nano-materials, and specialty steel); and optoelectronic display technology and manufacturing (OLED).

Section C focuses on incubating new and hi-tech small- and medium-sized enterprises (SMEs).

Q: What other industries or segments are you interested in?

A: KSND is looking to attract world Fortune 500 companies and world leading enterprises that are involved in OLED, solar energy equipment manufacturing and automobile electronics research and development.

Q: What are the strongest selling points of KSND?

A: SMEs and industries that are looking at China's domestic

market, need financial, legal, licensing and marketing support. They also need logistic services and distribution assistance. KSND is able to provide all of this. As a service provider, our main efforts are devoted to developing our SMEs directly with financial advice, technical assistance, supplier arrangements, human resource recruitment and economic matchmaking. We are one of the few SEZs that are concentrating on SMEs as a means of developing innovation.

Q: You seem to have a diverse portfolio of project areas, how does it work in practice?

A: Thanks to its multi-functional investment platforms, KSND is booming. It has formed a unique developing mode which can be described as "multiple parks within one zone." The Privately-owned Science Park, the Jiangsu Mould Industrial Experimentation Park, the National Hi-Tech Industrial Service Center, the Tsinghua Science and Technology Park, the Grand Economic & Trade Area, the Trade & Logistics Park, the American Industrial Village, and the Modern Service Industry Park—all of them have been built one after the other. It is a great source of pride to us that we have been recognized as one of the leading hi-tech intensive industrial enterprise zones in China. Our success is due to our commitment to foster innovation while providing a low-cost environment.

Author's Note

We discussed Rosemary's recent experience in Maryland and her thoughts about US economic crisis. Although SME incubation is an old topic in the US and Europe, it is still evolving in China. She made it clear that KSND is open for business and would welcome companies with new technology or products. After touring a number of their factories and talking to a number of the CEOs, I was impressed with the diversity of businesses that were using the park to build their businesses. Rosemary speaks excellent English and would be someone I would talk to if I was looking to locate a new business in China.

Promoting the brand—Kunshan New and Hi-Tech Industrial Development Zone (KSND)

Departments and Bureaus

Kunshan's success has been built up over time using the coordinated efforts of its departments and bureaus. Issues like infrastructure, urban planning, incorporation, licensing and coordination are handled by a variety of departments that work like a well-coordinated ballet. While most companies that have come to Kunshan have no idea of the complexity of the efforts going on behind the scenes, the story of how Kunshan's departments work together is the meat and potatoes of its success. Great ideas are wonderful but execution is the key. The following interviews will give you an idea of how these departments see themselves and how they work together.

Interview with Mr. Du Lixin

Du Lixin, Director-General of Kunshan City Development and Reform Commission

While not involved in the day-to-day execution of policies, the City Development and Reform Commission is one of the most powerful planning groups in government. In essence, it represents the planning arm of Beijing. Having contact with this office is important if you are trying to anticipate opportunities within the Chinese domestic market and what new policies may affect your industry.

Q: You are a unique part of government, what's the role of the Kunshan City D&R Commission?

A: The D&R Commission is a unique department and important adviser in Chinese government. We provide planning, guidance, direction and services to the city's economic, social and industrial development. We make and submit Kunshan's five-year plan based on the National D&R Commission's guidelines and central government's five-year plans.

In our supervisory role, we have some leeway to be creative and we often make adjustments as things develop. Our role is to facilitate development which follows the national development policies and guidelines. Sometimes, the central planning was not very detailed and overly rigid, often failing to take into account different local conditions. Today, the central government relies on local bureaus to report progress and suggestions as part of their eyes and ears. We therefore are as interested in new solutions as we are in compliance.

Q: Each city in China receives the same guidelines from the central government, why is Kunshan able to achieve constant success?

A: Four main reasons: outstanding leadership, consistent national policies (east

Up-scale housing—Sun Island golf villas

coast to be the first opening-up area), special location (next to Shanghai), and early emphasis on attracting talents and capital (comprehensive perspective).

Q: What have been the keys to your Bureau's success?

A: There are several examples of how Kunshan was identified and seized opportunities that explain its success.

In 1990, the central government authorized the development of the Shanghai Pudong EDZ. At first, people in Kunshan thought this was terrible news. But after communicating with a number of experts and scholars, we developed a plan to take advantage of the new development. The key was to study Pudong and then cater to those industries we could serve better. In the end, Pudong's development actually opened the global window for Kunshan.

Kunshan hired Mckinsey & Co. to help develop ideas for a new EDZ. It was an unusual move by Kunshan because very few county-level cities had ever hired a foreign expert of McKinsey's caliber before. Mckinsey assigned experts from the US and Malaysia to work on this project and presented a complete proposal. Rather than accepting the proposal as a whole, Kunshan studied it carefully and selected only those parts of the plans which made sense. As a result, Kunshan's Huaqiao International Service Business Park became the first EDZ to create its business model around the outsourcing industry in China.

Q: How do you see Kunshan's future industrial system developing?

A: We consult closely with the Shanghai Academy of Social Sciences about what and where to develop. Based on our studies, we see four major industries as key to Kunshan's future: distinctive electronics and IT (mainly consumer electronics, including laptop, camera, cell phone and accessories, etc.); equipment manufacturing (large construction machinery, such as excavator, crane and weight carrier, etc.); service outsourcing; and new industries (new material, new energy, new pharmacy and new biotech).

We believe a comprehensive geographic development plan is essential. We have observed that many Chinese cities copy trends blindly without thinking strategically about logical locations and differentiation. We have therefore suggested that Kunshan develop its industries carefully according to a comprehensive plan, which can be summarized as follows:
- Equipment manufacturing: northern Kunshan;
- IT: along the highway towards Shanghai;
- Outsourcing: two ends of the highway to Shanghai (Huaqiao & Bacheng); and
- Tourism: northern and southern Kunshan (Yangcheng Lake, Dianshan Lake and old villages like Zhouzhuang).

We are hopeful that other Chinese cities will see some value in our efforts and adapt our thinking to their situation.

Interview with Mr. Xu Zhenmin

Xu Zhenmin, Director-General of Kunshan Urban Planning Bureau

Quality of life—A garden in the city

Planning bureaus are often overlooked by businesses which is a big mistake. Infrastructure, logistics and the future quality of your life will depend on this bureau. A thoughtful, well-run planning bureau is one of the best indicators of the health and prospects of a city, and it is one of the first places you should go to when doing your business location intelligence. Power, roads, water and sewer are going to depend on how well this department functions. Most Chinese cities will greet you with the proverbial "no problem" approach to all your voiced needs. But until you understand their delivery capabilities, you are asking for trouble. All the upfront sweet talk is not going to resolve your lack of gas, electricity and access to your new facility.

Main function: follow national and provincial planning, responsible for Kunshan's urban planning (organize, compare, discuss, compile, apply and register), permission for resorts, historic zones and cultural zones, feasibility studies of locations for large construction projects, licensing for new buildings, roads, pipelines and other engineering projects as well as repairs, construction supervision, land use right transfers (tender and bidding), and regulation of urban planning, surveying and GIS.

Q: How would you explain the function of your bureau?

A: We are in charge of strategic planning and current const-ruction guidelines. We just finished Kunshan's Master Plan (2009-2030). The core contents of the overall plan are:

- Metropolitan development (create an infrastructure environment which can support tertiary industries and the people who will work in them);
- Modernization (introduce more efficient systems like light rail); and
- Sustainable development (new model development guidelines, industrial transformation and upgrading).

Q: What process do you use to create and approve new plans?

A: Usually, the following steps are followed:

- Planning: the planning took two years based on information gathered by the department from both other parts of the government and physical environment;
- Proposal: designed by experts (Chinese and foreign);
- Public review: locals are asked to look at the plan in terms of its responsiveness to the people's needs;
- Revisions: as necessary;
- Submittal: to Kunshan City Party Committee;
- Referral: to Kunshan City People's Congress for approval; and
- Final approval: Jiangsu provincial government.

We collaborate closely with the urban planning institutes of Shanghai Municipality & Jiangsu Province to make sure Kunshan will be connected with Shanghai's future development as well as part of Jiangsu's city-county system. The project manager is the deputy director-general of Jiangsu Provincial Construction Bureau who's in charge of urban planning.

Q: What is your relationship with Shanghai?

A: In the past, we depended on Shanghai; at present, we plan to blend into Shanghai; and in the future, we plan to serve Shanghai.

Q: Can you give an example of how your planning function has been used in Kunshan's economic development?

A: We have moved many old factories to suburban locations to free up land for the Kunshan New and High-Tech District and a number of research facilities. Companies that were moved were transitioned to new land and compensated for their facilities. Due to the age of a number of facilities, it was a win-win situation because most were in need of expansion space for their growing operations. The negotiations are handled through consultation and the companies have the right to take their case to provincial court if they feel they have not been treated fairly. To date, no one has taken such action. The system works because the government is very protective of its pro-development reputation and makes extraordinary efforts to settle matters fairly in ways all sides can agree on.

Interview with Mr. Zhang Zhenyue

Zhang Zhenyue, Director-General of Kunshan Bureau of Commerce

As a foreigner, this bureau is both a doorway and a resource, as they will interpret the central government policies and be in charge of processing and registering your company.

Q: What is your function?

A: Our main function: overall regulation, service and supervision of international trade and cooperation. We provide guidance and planning for devising strategies to bring in foreign capital; we study and research international law issues, WTO rules and other regulations and provide advice to the city government on matters involving foreign trade. We are in charge of issuing licenses to foreign trading companies involved in importing and exporting, agent licenses (sales and logistics, ads and exhibitions); we work with other departments to check technology import contracts and for-eign-invested projects applications. We supervise the complaint center; organize trade fairs and promotion events, issue invitation to bid on mechanical and electronic products and train people to handle international trade issues.

Q: How does your function relate to the central government?

A: I just came back from Beijing. The purpose was to visit the new leaders of the Foreign Capital Department in the Ministry of Commerce. Kunshan is the first county-level city to be invited to meet the new leaders, which shows how well Kunshan is regarded by the central authorities.

Q: Can you list what you think are Kunshan's most important achievements?

A: Kunshan was a well-known agricultural area in the 1970s. It produced 50 percent of the rice and 75 percent of the edible oil for the entire Suzhou area. However, Kunshan was last in total economic development of all six of Suzhou's counties in the 1980s. Former leaders realized the importance of developing secondary industries. The initial strategy was to try to attract military factories from western China and foreign businesses. As a result, the first WOFE was founded in 1985. In the 1990s, Kunshan actively interpreted the "opening-up policy" Deng had urged. Today, there are 5,800 overseas companies in Kunshan (60 percent are from Taiwan; 900 are European and 600 are from the US, Japan and the Republic of Korea). Total committed investment is over 50 billion US dollars (the actual capital in place is over 15 billion US dollars to date). In 2008, we did 61.3 billion US dollars worth of import and export (38.6 billion dollars were in export). We are the No. 1 county-level city in China, the No. 20 largest import and export area in China, the No.10 import and export city as well as the No.8 export city. Exports increased 1.2 percent even in the first 11 months of 2009. We are No.4 out of all the 54 national EDZs, with the No. 1 being Tianjin, No.2 being Suzhou (in cooperation with Singapore), and No. 3 being Guangzhou (ranked by the Ministry of Commerce in 2009).

Technology in action—Solar/wind powered streetlights on Huanqing Road

Q: Why has Kunshan been so successful?

A: Our leaders were forward thinkers. They developed comprehensive integrated strategies and used practical approaches to implement them. We have natural advantages in terms of our proximity to Shanghai, excellent transportation systems and access, including roads, rail, canals, rivers, air and ports. We have a great environment for living and business, clean air, less traffic, low-housing prices, beautiful parks, excellent cultural amenities, comprehensive infrastructure and great hard-working people. Our government service model has been considered as a demonstration model in China. We are a low-cost, high-efficiency area that is dedicated to overcoming any barrier which prevents us from achieving our assigned goals.

Because we have taken the time to explain our plans and educate our people, we have their support and help. We have been lucky to have outstanding leaders like Mr. Wu, who had worked in the National Planning Commission. We have also been fortunate in being able to attract many educated young leaders, especially from western China during the 1980s. It helps that we work under unswerving central policies that have allowed us to drive our economy with foreign capital, expand our domestic business and develop a new service model. We have a strong team spirit which includes never being satisfied and always looking for the next opportunity. We have always been prepared to find and seize opportunities.

Q: Can you cite something that illustrates what you're saying?

A: Yes, it is kind of a case study which illustrates how we think about and deal with the economic crisis cycle.

Kunshan has consistently benefited during times of crisis. In 1998, as the result of the economic displacement caused by the Asian financial crisis, Kunshan successfully attracted Taiwanese electronic companies. In 2003, during the SARS epidemic, Kunshan city government quickly organized an investment promotion event in Hong Kong just one day after the travel restrictions were lifted. The people in Hong Kong were very impressed and responded favorably. It set us apart because, at a time when others worried, we saw and chased the opportunities presented. In 2006, we anticipated that there might be another financial crisis. After lots of discussion with higher government departments and consulting companies, Kunshan government decided to use the crisis to facilitate a transformation of our economic structure towards tertiary industries such as BPO (business process outsourcing), financial services, and modern logistics.

Q: What does Kunshan need to do next?

A: Kunshan needs to take its message to the global stage, just like the "Made in China" ads which were aired by the Ministry of Commerce. We need to follow their example and figure out new ways to attract the types of businesses that can move our economy into the next phase.

We also need to be clearer about our motivations. Our economic activities are just tools to make our economy stronger, so we can extend the opportunities of a prosperous society to all. The creation of a scientific development and sustainable society is the goal, but to achieve it each new generation must be prepared to take on the work that is necessary to create and maintain the goal. For many of us, we recognize that our most important responsibility is to prepare the way for the next generation.

Interview with Mr. Shen Yuexin

Shen Yuexin, Director-general, Bureau of Science and Technology

This bureau is essential to companies with leading edge development needs. It is also one of the must-visit departments companies should have on their list when doing their due diligence. With huge resources and direct authority, it can be one of your most valuable resources. Again everything depends on the ability of the department to understand and assist your efforts.

Q: How would you describe your main functions?

A: Our main functions are national and local strategy and regulation, to create annual and long-term science and technology plans and budget. We also guide, manage and promote agricultural science and technology industrialization in rural areas, IP protection and related publicity, statistics and awards of science and technology development, facilitate cooperation between business and academics, and provide suggestions for attracting talented people.

Q: What is the main role your bureau plays in assisting companies, can you provide examples?

A: The Bureau of Science and Technology is a very important strategic department of the Kunshan city government. Because we are in the process of transforming from low-end manufacturing to a high-end value-added economy, we are responsible for developing and implementing policies which further Kunshan's goals.

We have a case study involving Netmarch Technologies, a software company, which serves as an example of what we are looking for. It was founded by a returned Kunshan student who was educated in the US. We helped him capitalize his hi-tech company with a 50,000-yuan investment. Today, the company is valued at more than 100 million yuan. It's a successful example of how to combine individual efforts and government support. He was particularly impressed because we picked him up at the airport when he was coming in to talk to us about his initial ideas. We have found that it is often the small things which show sincerity and we have used this to our advantage.

Q: How do you encourage innovation and protect IP?

A: In order to encourage innovation, Kunshan created a searchable information database, which is available to local companies, so they can research their ideas and create their patent applications more thoroughly.

We regularly provide patent application fees, capital and legal assistance to any companies that are filing patents or involved in IP infringement disputes.

We provide regular free training and promotion events to publicize new policies, like the requirements necessary to qualify for economic incentives. In addition to national subsidies, we also issue local subsidies to facilitate innovations.

We sponsor a regular joint scientific innovation conference where major city leaders, as well as representatives from every related government department, including science and technology, human resources, finance, industrial and commercial, and economic and trade bureaus. Thanks to their attendance, we can coordinate our activities and programs. Given the nature of our efforts, we have found that joint efforts and combined resources are the key to results.

We administer an innovation budget which is passed by Kunshan City People's

Congress each year. In 2009, the total amount was about 1 billion yuan, 40 percent of which will be used as special fund to support innovation, IP protection and R&D facilities. Each year, we use 100 million yuan as incentive bonuses to attract talented innovators and technical professionals needed by companies in Kunshan. Over the next three years, we will spend 1 billion yuan to purchase equipment for the Industrial Technology Research Institute which is under construction.

Q: How do you connect business and academics? Examples?

A: I have a quick case study which demonstrates how we work to move something from research to market: We created a high-level direct cooperation with Qiu Yong, a Tsinghua University scientist who started Visionox (OLED). Visionox's new technology has enabled us to create a new Chinese OLED industry by turning academic research into marketable products. Our goal is to be able to recognize and help promising technologies which can be used in products to support our manufacturing strengths. Establishing good relations with academics who often are puzzled by the business aspects of their discoveries is one of our goals. We believe our way of doing things and our success has become a kind of brand that we can use in our future development.

Author's Note

The average foreigner who opens a business in Kunshan will never meet Mr. Zhang, Mr. Du, Mr. Xu and Mr. Shen as they will be assigned a project manager who will be their one point of contact. But issues, when they come up, will be discussed and solved, mostly behind the scenes, by these people and their bureaus. The guts of every city are the people who carry its business forward, taking care of the paperwork and making decisions as needed. What surprised me most about my interview with this group was their emphasis on flexibility. A bureau in China not only functions as a local entity, but also reports up to the province and eventually the central government. With a multiple reporting structure, I was expecting to find the kind of rigid bureaucratic attitudes which seem to come with entrenched lifers, instead I encountered a group of engaged civil servants who seemed to constantly stress the need for flexibility and case by case analysis. In the end it dawned on me that most foreign companies were missing out by not getting to know these people and their functions. The amount of information these bureaus have about pending developments and government policies is a virtual goldmine in a country like China. My suggestion is that if you are looking at setting up a business in a Chinese city, one of the first places to start your due diligence is at the local government bureaus. Make an appointment at their office, look around, and you will get a pretty good idea what kind of ship you are signing on to. For my part it was interesting to note the positive differences between my experiences in Kunshan and other places in China.

Rural Voices

Unlike the US where economic development is the objective, in Kunshan and in China, economic development is just a tool in the struggle to create a "sustainable and harmonious society." It seems to be the reason that "serving the people" takes on perhaps a bit more urgency and meaning than in other systems. Unlike our arrangement which vacillates between political parties, the Communist Party stands alone. It is a double-edged sword which allows the country to make and implement its policies much more quickly than in the US but makes the Party ultimately responsible for the results. Whereas in the US, we expect the government to create and enforce the rules of society, in China the people believe it is the government's responsibility to produce and maintain a better society.

At a time when many rural people are facing greater income and benefit disparities with their urban cousins, Kunshan has achieved remarkable results. Aided in part by lease sales of collective lands to factories, commercial and residential developers, and in part by new benefit policies, many rural residents now enjoy a better quality of life than their urban counterparts. But, it is not all wine and roses. Many

Bridges from the past to the future—Rural Kunshan village

of the early lease sales were to factories which created environmental side effects which will take time and money to repair.

Interview with Mr. Qian Junxiong

Qian Junxiong, current deputy secretary-general of Kunshan City People's Government and director-general of Rural Work Office of Kunshan City Party Committee

Q: What has Kunshan's growth meant for its rural people?

A: Their income levels have increased dramatically. Our ratio of urban to rural income is 1.77:1, the smallest in Jiangsu and probably China. The confirmation comes from the farmers themselves, 76 percent of whom believe that they are now well-off.

Rural people now enjoy better living standards as their standard of living and life styles have become closer to urban people.

Rural people now have insurance and social benefits. Kunshan has extended a full set of personal, medical and crop insurance to farmers, making their lives more secure and comfortable.

In terms of the environment, the government is working to rectify the damage done in the earlier years when pollution from factories created issues. Today, the government is using more green technology and planning techniques to protect the water and natural areas.

To assist in the transition from rural to urban, the government has provided free vocational education and skill training courses to farmers and encouraged those with the interest to start their own businesses.

Q: Every government employee I have talked to seems to always include a reference to the plight of farmers. Part of it I assume is the empathy they feel for a life style which most are only one-generation-apart form. Will these concerns continue or do you think they will fade as people become more urbanized?

A: I do not think so. The structure of our system and the central policy directions we receive are very clear. You can not just forget about the 800 million rural people. If someone is not interested in this type of work, it is doubtful that he can be a very good leader or Party member. We have a long rural tradition in Kunshan, careful planning, pragmatic action and hard work are part of that heritage and part of the way we go about our life and work. As long as the natural beauty of our water towns, lakes and rivers exists, we will always be reminded of our ties to the land.

Interview with Mr. Zhang Guishen

Zhang Guishen, retired, Jinhua New Village

Q: What have been the greatest changes during the last 20 years?

A: Our family income. There are five people in my family. Every year, each person is given 2.5 tons of liquid gas, four bags of rice (200 kilos) and other food like fish. The total annual revenue of our family reaches 250,000 yuan (150,000 from salaries and 100,000 from our small business). I would never have believed that I and my family would be in this position.

Mr. Zhang Guishen

The other major change was a bridge which was built partly with funds from a land lease and individual contributions by village families. In the past, the village was surrounded by water in all directions. After the construction of the bridge, we have been able to develop businesses and work in factories, giving us many more opportunities.

Another change is that we are all covered by social, crop and medical insurance (70 percent of medical fees will be covered by government) and every farmer can receive 1,000 yuan as pension and 700 yuan as subsidies (physical commodities) each month when he or she retires. We are also allowed to use small pieces of land for growing crops if we feel like it.

Mr. Wang Dongquan

Interview with Mr. Wang Dongquan

Wang Dongquan, retired, Jinhua New Village

Q: What changes have you noticed most in your family? How do you like your current life?

A: There are eight people in my family, but my wife and I are the only ones living in the village, the children live in larger towns. I worked for the last several decades in Jinhua Village, my wife was a village doctor. Right now is the best time in my life, a time of prosperity. I feel that we have achieved a harmonious society at least in our village and area.

The two big changes in our village and family life were the creation of the factory and the building of a bridge. The factory gave us jobs and changed our financial condition. The bridge changed the nature of our village by connecting us physically to the outside world. People could live in the village and easily work in jobs elsewhere. Both events brought changes especially to the local economy which developed rapidly as transportation improved.

Q: What about the life of the other people of this village? I notice many are old. What will happen in the future?

A: After many years of hard work, we older people are finally able to enjoy our lives. The village built entertainment facilities for us which we use daily. We are now covered by medical and social insurance and, together with the lease fees we receive from the collective we are able to relax without worrying about our future. Although most of our children work in the towns, we old people prefer our life in the village.

Q: What changes have you noticed most since the "opening up"?

A: In Chairman Mao's time, there were three huge gaps: gap between workers and farmers; gap between cities and villages; and gap between mental work and physical work. Today, the gaps have almost disappeared in this area. Truthfully, many feel that our life in the village is much better than life in the urban areas where everyone is always in a hurry and you have to deal with traffic. I never thought I would see the changes China has gone through in my life. There were many hardships but things have turned out better than I ever expected, so I believe our sacrifices were worth it.

The changes are not only in our material existence. As people's financial conditions improved their tastes changed. We now have basketball, gate ball, dancing, singing teams,

a card and chess room, a medical clinic, internet access and even our own TV station. Even as a child, I would never have dreamed that such things were even possible.

Q: What will happen to rural life, will it disappear as you know it?

A: The younger generations born after the founding of New China has never had to go through really difficult times and they might find the life of a farmer too hard. They have different cultural tastes and hobbies. People have different perspectives, not everyone appreciates rural life. With the help of more efficient modern agricultural equipment and technologies, we don't need everyone in the village to work in the fields. I do not think people will miss the hard work, but the country life has many other rewards which can not be found in city life.

Q: Who put together the investment of the first bridge?

A: The investment for the first bridge was put together by the villagers committee (80 percent), the city government (15 percent), and local donations. I donated 2,000 yuan as a representative of the local people who were working in companies or factories. The total investment was 1.6 million yuan. It was a very big project for our little village and it has brought big changes.

Q: What do you think of the old planned economy system?

A: I'm not fond of the planned economy system: it did not provide incentives. Every farmer had the same life. After Deng's "opening-up" policy, individuals had many different options. For example, in Jinhua Village, farmers put their investment together with the villagers committee to build factories, and then everyone shared the profits just like stock shares.

Q: What do you think about China's future?

A: I am confident of China's future. Although the young people have no experience of suffering, they heard those stories from old people. Passing on perspectives is a great Chinese tradition. Young people in Jinhua treat their parents very well, so their children will treat them well.

Author's Note

Mr. Zhang and Mr. Wang are into their 60's, they were young when the new People's Republic was still young and they have seen the best and worst of times. Their village hall is a picturesque new structure that borrows heavily from Chinese traditional architecture. It has a formal meeting room and a few offices, but much of it seems to be a community center which was being used by old and young alike the day I visited. Having been shown the pictures of the village 20 and 30 years ago it is an unbelievable transformation. Much of the wealth of the village has come through the leasing of its lands to commercial ventures or through cooperative commercial ventures involving the village—village residents and often outside investors. Since industrial land leases last only 50 years, the village can expect an influx of new income in the years to come.

Kunshan is as usual one of the first cities to be offering a new comprehensive retirement and medical program, paid for from its urban economic activities. It remains to be seen whether these benefits will be extended throughout China. Kunshan can afford it now because of China's current residency, or *hukou*, system which ties all social benefits, including free schooling, to the place you are registered in. At least three times as many people work in Kunshan as those who have *hukou*, and in many cases those registered in Kunshan actually live elsewhere. The central government has been in the process of looking at the residency issue for quite some time. But it will not be easily solved. The resources required to provide services would overwhelm those cities whose populations are dominated by migrant workers, including Beijing and Shanghai.

In many ways, my visit was like walking into a Norman Rockwell painting, complete with expressive subjects and an idealized setting, but paintings can only capture a moment in time. What Kunshan is able to do may not be possible in other areas. So it will remain to be seen. I visited only five villages in Kunshan, each had a distinctive flavor and setting. In each, there was the unmistakable bustle of purpose, energy and hope. In judging what the Kunshan Way has done for its people, it is clear that its economic success is being used to pursue social goals and, if that is their measure of success, the Kunshan Way is successful.

On the right:
The houses have changed but nature remains the same—Rural Kunshan

The Kunshan Human Resources Department,
matching people and businesses

If you are going to do business in Kunshan or another city you should understand some rudimentary things about their model of city government; the differences in structure, the role of the Party, the function of the government, the basic steps to incorporating and getting licensed and the experiences of others who have come to Kunshan.

Political and Administrative Structure of Cities in China

Too often people look at China's political/ideological systems without attempting to understand what they mean in practice. Ideology may be the elephant in the room, but if you are trying to do business in China, you need to understand how things work and who are involved.

If you come to China for business, you will meet a bewildering array of officials at different levels of the Party and government. Figuring out who you need to deal with and why is just as crucial in China as anywhere else. Part of the problem is that your Chinese intermediary or partner, if you have one, is not always clear either. Unless they are locals, more often than not, they are relying on a "friend" for information.

In Kunshan this is less of an issue because, as a smaller city with a mature service model, you will be taken care of quickly and efficiently, but if you are in a different or larger city you need to know the basics of the relationship between the Party and the government, the structure of the bureaus, departments and commissions, what they are responsible for, their goals and decision-making process and the people involved who are vital to your business. Yes, it can be opaque but unless you come to grips with these issues you will be walking blind.

The Western Model

Western city government models differ greatly depending on the country. In terms of the spectrum of central vs. local control the US has probably the most locally focused system. In the US cities have only those powers granted to them by the state and states have all powers not vested in the federal government. Although, there are five different general city models they share a common structure; elected representatives preside over the bureaucracy and appointed functionaries. Checks and balances are set up in the city's constitution/charter, which specifies which officers and bodies have control over budget, administration and accounting. The norm is a power-sharing arrangement which entrusts administration to an executive entity and oversight to a body of elected members. Ultimately elections are the final check.

Few qualifications other than age, citizenship and a majority of the people who chose to vote are necessary to be elected. Even a criminal record is not an absolute obstacle to holding elected office. Once elected, the majority of time is spent addressing constituent issues and responding to crises as they occur. Budgets and control are the main areas of political contention. National policies and direction are only considered important if it involves funds or local issues. Political party affiliation is extremely loose. While elected officials can bear the brunt of the electorate's unhappiness over economic and social conditions, at election time, their actual power is more reactive than proactive.

The main areas of responsibility are: land use through urban planning and zoning, public works and infrastructure, public safety, public amenities, enforcement of local laws and requirements, tax collection, internal administration and general promotion of the area. In the US for example a city of 600,000 would qualify as the 23rd largest city in the nation.

From Britain to Kunshan—TESCO's, grocery and general merchandising

The Chinese Model

In China, provinces and provincial-level municipalities have only those powers granted to them by the central government. There are over 450 Chinese cities with populations over 500,000. Cities are grouped into five categories: municipalities (there are four municipalities Beijing, Shanghai, Tianjin and Chongqing); sub-provincial-level cities (15); provincial capital cities; prefecture-level cities and county-level cities. Beyond that there are townships, towns, villages and collectives. While there are many different types of cities, there is only one government form which is a city government bureaucracy, which is run mostly by Party members and overseen by the Party on behalf of the people. Checks and balances, power and control are handled by the local Party oversight of the government and the next higher level of the Party and government which, for Kunshan, is Suzhou. The ultimate oversight is exercised by the central government and the Party Central Committee.

To be in the Party, you must be a Party member; to be in the municipal government you need not. In practice, the overwhelming majority are, especially in the higher positions. Party affiliation is strong and although within the Party there are vast differences of opinion, when it comes to public pronouncements all members are expected to adhere to the Party line. Many people join the Party while in college and it is seen as both an ideological and career commitment.

As a government official and/or Party member, you are directly responsible for carrying out the central government and Party's directives and achieving assigned goals. Your career will depend on your ability to get things done and the perceptions of your superiors. With over 70 million Party members contending for higher spots on the pyramid Party life is brutally competitive. To advance you need to produce results, make friends, refrain from making mistakes and be very lucky.

The plus, under the current Communist system, is there's no question of continuity, but the negative is there is no one else to blame if things go wrong. This power responsibility equation means that those in Beijing, who sit at the top of the pyramid, are under constant pressure to produce results

and as usual pressure flows down hill. The one advantage they have is that the government holds powerful cards and can use them to accomplish desired ends. It is why, rather than cheerleading, Chinese cities are allowed, and often encouraged, to make direct investments in or own and operate strategic businesses. They also have the power to own equity, engage in joint ventures, offer direct economic incentives, guarantee and make loans (indirectly).

They can use their powers to vigorously promote their cities and aggressively pursue foreign direct investment (FDI). They also directly regulate incorporation, licensing, inspection, public safety, land, zoning, construction and infrastructure. Since land is in essence held in trust for the people and leased out, cities have very strong control over urban planning and zoning. If an area is needed for an economic or public purpose, the only issue is compensation.

Bottom line, Chinese cities have the same responsibilities as their US counterparts, but they have more tools and take a more direct hand in all aspects of their social and economic development. The challenge is that with more power, more is expected. Unlike US and other Western cities there is no political pressure relief valve and therefore the pressure is constant and intense.

The Municipal Government Structure

The chart shows the departments/bureaus and their levels which fall under the municipal government structure. Most of it corresponds roughly with departments in US cities, but be careful about assuming anything. It is best to use someone who is familiar with the particular municipality you are interested in, because although things are generally the same you can not afford to make a mistake. The main purpose of this information is so you can attempt to understand the often bewildering business cards you are handed when you attend meetings.

Also remember that every city has several vice-mayors who have separate areas of responsibility. Meeting with a vice-mayor can be good, or just feel good. The large numbers of delegations which come to China on a daily basis means that there are a number of officials who spend the majority of their time greeting foreign dignitaries. Unless there has been careful preparation and/or there is something to sign which will involve an investment, do not count on meetings with the heavy hitters.

Chinese cities differ only slightly in their organizational structures from one to the next; the main difference will be in who holds which position, or combination of positions, their individual and collective capabilities. The way internal organization is handled is similar to the way political parties in the US organize themselves when they have a majority. Chairmanships and committee assignments are parceled out based on a combination of seniority, political clout and capabilities by higher and generally more senior members of the Party. As in the US, a unified façade can often hide intense differences of opinion and competitions for power. Like water polo, what you see may look graceful from above, but beneath the water there is often a different reality.

Commissions, bureaus and departments report to the local Party and municipal leaders as well as to the next higher level of commissions, bureaus and depart-

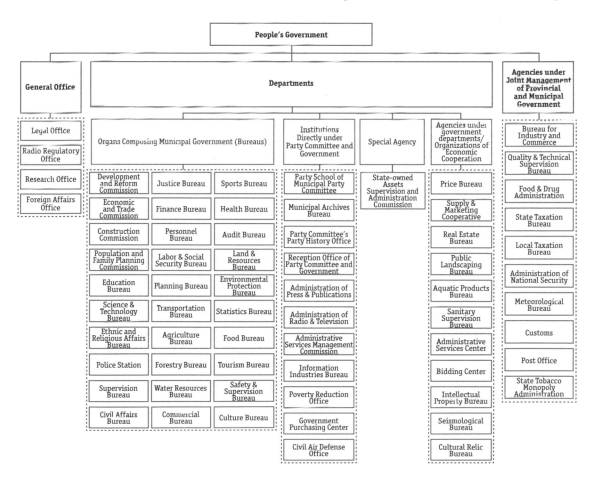

ments. Cities are the base of an operational pyramid whose top is in Beijing. County-level cities, like Kunshan, are the front line of the structure; they disseminate and collect information to and from every town, village, state-owned enterprise (SOE), cooperative, public institution, state-funded school, etc. The major difference is that their informational responsibilities are linked to their management role. Ideology is important but capability and results are crucial. Each layer of the pyramid relies on the lower level to make them look good; they are therefore under intense pressure to produce results. As can be imagined, your inability to do so will have an effect on the careers of those above you and consequently on yours.

Yes Minister

Unfortunately, in some areas this leads to a "Yes Minister" scenario (British sitcom of the early 80's which pitted ambitious cabinet ministers against an entrenched and risk-averse bureaucracy), where ambitious Chinese leaders eager to show their capabilities, are forced to depend on teams which might not share their enthusiasm for the extra work and risks involved. Like all bureaucracies, there are often too many who have the experience but have lost their zeal, or who have the zeal but lack experience. Creating an effective team is often the ultimate test. The reality is that in the best case scenario the able leader will be promoted within three to five years to a higher position. It in part explains the importance of friendship (*guanxi*) in the Chinese workplace; the assumption that even when someone leaves the connection and obligation will continue.

Do Your Homework

If possible, before you meet a group of Chinese officials you should try to understand their positions and powers. It will give you a better idea of what they are thinking and where you are. A meeting with a Party secretary who is fully briefed on the situation and backed by an assortment of high-, middle- and ground-level functionaries from the government side means business, a meeting headed by a bureau chief (director-general) whose responsibilities have nothing to do with your project means something else. To get a general idea, you need to understand the relationship between the Party and the municipal government and the major bureaus and what they do. The list is not meant to be exhaustive but just to give you an idea. The second thing you need to do is carefully prepare for meetings, send them your information and an outline of what you want to do and ask them to do the same. Ask pointedly for the background and current position of the people you will be meeting with and give them the same information about yourself and your team. With thousands of choices where you could invest in China, if you have a good idea, funding and a plan you are in the catbird seat.

A view of Kunshan's Huaqiao International Business District (25 km to the center of Shanghai)

Kunshan's Administrative Service Center, one stop shopping for doing businesses in Kunshan

City Government and Party Components

The overall system has four main components:

- The Municipal Party Committee (composed of Party members who act as an executive for the people's congress and are responsible for reviewing the actions of Party members and the local government);
- The Municipal People's Congress (the legislative body which has the power to make rules and laws within the scope allowed by the central government);
- The Municipal Government Offices (the administrative body, elected by the Municipal People's Congress, which fulfills the planning and administrative functions of the government);
- The Municipal Committee of the Chinese People's Political Consultative Conference (CPPCC, a consultative body led by mostly retired Party members and non-Party local notables, including representatives from businesses, the professions, law enforcement, the judiciary and education. It reviews laws and makes suggestions but does not have rule-making authority. Party membership is not required).

The confusing part is that officials will often hold multiple positions in a number of the government and Party bodies simultaneously, which is why the power structure often looks so circular.

The Party

The relationship of the Communist Party to the structure of government is one area that few people, even "old China hands", seem to understand. Yet, this relationship is the single most important aspect of China's development. Rather than discounting it as an ideological concept, we need to understand how it works.

Ideologically: the Party is in charge of guiding the development and education of all government and state-owned enterprises (SOEs, enterprises owned by cities, provinces and the central government).

Politically: all government, state-owned enterprises and public institutions must follow the Party's direction, strategy and policies.

Organizationally: the Party selects and supervises all government, SOE and public institution employees. All employees are part of a management unit and all management units report to a Party committee.

The Municipal Party Committee

As the most powerful and important decision-making organization, the Standing Committee of the Municipal Party Committee generally consists of:

Party secretary of Municipal Party Committee;

Vice Party secretary (generally the mayor);

Vice Party secretary (in charge of Party affairs);

Executive vice-mayor;

Secretary of Commission for Discipline Inspection;

Director of Organization Department;

Director of Publicity Department;

Secretary of Politics and Law Committee;

Secretary-general of Municipal Party Committee;

Selected vice-mayors;

Director of United Front Work Department;

Party secretary(ies) of the city's most important district(s);

Commanding police officer;

Political commissar of any military sub-area in which the city is in.

The Commission for Discipline Inspection

The head of this commission (secretary) is generally a standing committee member of the Municipal Party Committee, which is in charge of all Party members' discipline issues. The Party Committee has the right to inspect, investigate and use Shuang Gui (fixed time and place to answer inquiries) for violations. Generally it directs and shares staff with Municipal Supervision Bureau (which is in charge of government departments and employees, the head of which is the deputy secretary of Commission for Discipline Inspection). The Supervision Bureau has the right to inspect all government-related departments and staff, whether they are Party members or not. The Party committee in theory only supervises Party members, but given that many members of the government are Party members and their close working relationship, if the Party has a reason to suspect that there is a problem with someone outside the Party it is probable that action will be taken by the municipal side. In some instances, there will be separate actions taken by both organizations.

The Party Committee Office

It manages the day-to-day coordination of Party efforts when they involve multiple Party committees. The head is the Secretary-General of Municipal Party Committee; they will generally also be a standing committee member of the Municipal Party Committee. Their main task is coordinating relationships and work efforts between different standing committees, their members and chairpersons. As a coordinating body, they have a large influence on how issues are resolved when competing interests are involved.

The Organization Department

The head of this department is a standing committee member of the Municipal Party Committee. It follows and enacts central government polices, regulations, and reform directives for human resource management and development. It's responsible for maintaining records on all Party officials, reviewing their performance and making recommendations for both administrative and legislative positions. It performs the same functions for SOEs and agricultural enterprises and collectives.

Publicity Department

It is generally headed by the publicity officer (the department is in charge of publicizing official information, central government theory, Party member education, including grading members understanding of relevant materials).It will have a number of sub-departments under it. The publicity officer is generally a member of the standing committee and is considered a half step higher than many of the other departments, offices and bureau heads.

Enterprise Office

It oversees and reviews SOEs and public institutions. While this might not affect you directly as a SME if you do business in China at one point or another, you will run into one of the legions of SOEs which dominate the domestic markets.

Culture and Education Office

Coordinates policy and publicity of cultural and educational institutions.

News Office

Officially known as Administration of Press and Publications, it coordinates media relations and official information efforts.

External Publicity Office

It is also called the Press Office of People's Government; it is in charge of the city's image promotion, news conferences and internet. This is also an example of a department which has overlapping roles on both the Party and municipal government sides.

United Front Work Department

Its main function is the research of united front work theory; it is a coordinating department which contacts Party and non-Party groups and representatives from outside the area to discuss strategy and policy for possible multi-party cooperation. It has additional responsibilities in the areas of:

Religion and Minority Ethnic Groups Issues and Efforts

This department overseas cooperative efforts not involving economic or political issues and identifies and recommends non-Party members who they believe should be included in government efforts.

Politics and Law Committee

A very powerful committee, the Party secretary of this committee is a standing committee member of Municipal Party Committee. Most of the time, he is also the director-general of police (on the municipal government side). This committee leads, manages and coordinates public security, prosecution and the courts. The organizations they supervise include the municipal police, People's Court, People's Procuratorate, the Justice Bureau and the Public Security Bureau (their mandate is ideological education, rating and selection of staff for promotion; they do not get involved with the day-to-day operations of the different departments, but the other members of the committee include the leaders of all four main Party components, so its advice is often sought when there are sensitive disputes.

Municipal Straight Institution Work Committee

The secretary of this committee is the secretary-general of Municipal Party Committee; the vice-secretary is usually the deputy secretary-general. The main function is to provide planning, supervision and services for Party building, anti-corruption education, spiritual civilization publicity and people's organizations work (such as trade union, women's federation).

Business Interviews and Case Studies

So far we have seen what Kunshan has to offer, listened to the government officials and the people who live and work in Kunshan, talked about the structure of government and what you need to know; the last pieces of the puzzle are listening to Kunshan's business men and women.

Goodbaby Child Products Co., Ltd. (Goodbaby)

Goodbaby is China's largest company specializing in the design, manufacture and distribution of children's products.

In 1989 the original workshop was affiliated with a middle school (literally it was a small business owned by a middle school); this was the rule rather than the exception under the unit management system in place at the time. Today elementary and high schools are not permitted to own or operate businesses not connected to their educational mission but cities, rural collectives and universities continue to invest, own and operate businesses and joint ventures. This is a strange concept for us; but, logically, since all land is held collectively and managed by the designated local government units, to build a factory, workshop, commercial or residential space, it had to be built with, or by, the unit that controlled the land.

No, the schools did not utilize the students as forced labor (although there have been instances during China's history when this occurred), nor was the workshop some type of smoke belching industrial behemoth, it was a small assembly shop. Disposable income at that time was extremely scarce; those who could afford a baby stroller wanted something with more than one use. After abandoning the idea of making inexpensive copies of Western designs, Mr. Song created a convertible stroller, walker, chair, and rocking crib which were an instant success. Today Mr. Song retains an 8 percent direct ownership of the company; the rest is spread among 200 current and former management employees.

Goodbaby has been certified by the Chinese government's commercial bureau as a leading Chinese brand. It dominates the sale of strollers in China and the US and it is the largest single seller in Europe. Americans would be more familiar with its US brands COSCO and/or Geobaby.

Now, the business is the No.1 in sales in China for 16 consecutive years (1993-2009), No.1 in sales in the US for 10 consecutive years (1999-2009), and No.1 in sales in Europe for three consecutive years (2006-2009).

Its rapid expansion has been fueled by a combination of strategic joint ventures, which provided the cash for its expansion, industry-leading design, efficient high-quality manufacturing processes and strategic marketing. The company's joint ventures, OEMs and proprietary manufacturing are supported by more than 10 specialized production facilities located in Kunshan.

The factories use state-of-the-art equipment, technology and industry-leading quality assurance systems. Located in the Kunshan Economic and Technology Development Zone, Goodbaby's industrial campus sits on 12,000 acres. The campus consists of the world's largest stroller factory, child bicycle factory, battery-operated toy car factory and wood factory. The campus is also home to its large injection molding and sewing factories. Goodbaby employs more than 16,000 skilled workers. It is ISO 9001 certified and has a solid experienced management team. It is in the process of building a 20,000-square-meter (215,000-square-feet) research and design building, conference center and showroom.

In addition to the work it does in China, Goodbaby's research and development team works closely with some of the world's leading international product design firms and safety institutes to design and create innovative, safe, comfortable, convenient, and fashionable products for infants, children and their parents. Goodbaby ranks No. 1 in the industry in terms of intellectual property, with over 4,000 Chinese and international patents. On any day thousands of its containers are in transit to destinations all over the world.

Recently, Goodbaby has started setting up its proprietary retail sales centers to bring its products directly to the marketplace.

Some of Goodbaby Group's products at their company showroom

Mr. Song Zhenghuan, Goodbaby Group's president and founder

Interview with Mr. Song Zhenghuan

President, Goodbaby Group

1949	Born in Jiangsu
1968-1973	Assigned to a rural work unit after high school
1973-1982	Attended University, majored in math
1982-1988	Hired by Lujia Town Middle School, Kunshan
1989	Assigned to work in Lujia Town Middle School's affiliated factory, changed the name to "Goodbaby"

Q: What are some of the things you would want people outside of China to know about Goodbaby?

A: Goodbaby is a family which has grown through the dedication of our workers, partners and suppliers. We are friends who have worked diligently together to create the Goodbaby brand.

I am proud that we have been recognized at home by our peers and by our leaders. The China Toy Association gave me its highest honor by naming me the most influential person in the industry (the only person who won this title in China).

Premier Wen Jiabao came to visit Goodbaby last year; he applauded our innovation and determination to be No. 1 in our industry. Both were great honors which show that when we work together there will be "no unconquerable difficulties".

I am also happy that we have been recognized abroad by firms like Boston Consulting Group, which ranked Goodbaby as one of the top "50 Local Dynamos in Rapidly Developing Economies" (note there were 15 Chinese companies on the list), and Ernst & Young, who named me Entrepreneur of the Year in 2007.

Q: How would you summarize Goodbaby's success?

A: We were successful because we constantly pursued better designs and more cost-efficient manufacturing processes.

Q: How did Goodbaby start in China?

A: In 1989, I was transferred from teaching middle school math to the small affiliated factory which was heavily in debt and had lost most of its employees and its entire technical staff. Rather than trying to copy existing products and compete on price, as the previous managers had, I decided that the only practical future for the company was to pursue innovation. Using my own ideas I created a practical "four-in-one" baby carrier which could be used as baby walker, rocking cradle and chair. It was an immediate success because it was a practical device which met the needs of Chinese families. The style is still being sold today and has cumulative sales of over 13 million.

Based on its initial success, Goodbaby became famous, but, cheaper imitations of our products started flooding the market. I decided the only response was to keep innovating; philosophically I believe that ultimately the race is not against others but "against yourself". In 1990, the first R&D team (three people) was formed in Goodbaby. By 1993, Goodbaby dominated the Chinese market with an array of products, which were in constant demand.

Q: Many Chinese companies make products as OEMs but few have had anywhere near the success you have had in not only taking your products to foreign markets but then dominating them. What strategy did you use to open up foreign markets for your products?

A: In 1994, I went to the US and started studying the market. The US market was different and there were a number of barriers which made entrance difficult, brand recognition, distribution and servicing were the most problematic. I left one staff person in the US to gather more information and returned to China. I was convinced that the best chance of entering the market was to create innovative designs which met the life styles and price points of the consumer market. With my design team we set to work. In 1995, I designed a baby swing which could be swung vertically and horizontally to keep children occupied. To deal with distribution I set up an agreement with an American partner, COSCO, an established brand with existing distribution channels, which had been pushed out of the market for various reasons. In 1996 Goodbaby started selling its products under the COSCO label and by 1999 it was No. 1 in the industry.

Innovative design created demand, but it was Goodbaby's cost points which drove the market. As designers the R&D team created designs which were not only practical, attractive and safe but also efficient and low-cost in terms of production. Combining the product with production design not only shortened development and manufacturing cycles, but created a continuous quality improvement loop which fed successive design development cycles.

Having had success in the US market, Goodbaby expanded its focus to include Europe. The European market was even more difficult than the American market, distribution was more segmented due to historical and language issues. Consumers were willing to spend more but were extremely focused on quality, safety and functionality. To understand the market, Goodbaby decided to work with established European design that knew the market. In 2003, we launched our first series of new products for the European market. Consumers reacted positively to the innovations offered because they suited their lifestyle and priorities. With smaller living environments, European consumers wanted stylish, collapsible, multifunctional stroller/baby carriers which were durable and safe. While price points were important we soon realized that for this market the added value came from quality design.

Q: Goodbaby has enjoyed phenomenal success in the world market. What is the key?

A: "Innovation has been our passport to the world's markets", our practice is to set up design facilities in every market we compete in. In addition to our current shops in Kunshan and the US, in 2007, we opened facilities in Holland and Japan which gives up the largest global design capabilities within the industry. When we started working in Europe in 2002, we collaborated with a number of Dutch design companies, it was a productive experience and has led to design collaborations with some of the world's leading design groups. Ultimately, we added our own design facilities so we could retain talent, maintain our competitive advantage and coordinate the process of integrating design with our manufacturing processes.

Q: How has the financial crisis affected Goodbaby?

A: For many the global meltdown was a setback, we saw it as an opportunity. The crisis has changed consumer specifications and price points. In 2009, we launched the largest number of new products in our history. In the absence of new products from our competitors, stores gave us expanded sales space and positioning, increasing our visibility and market share.

For example, when Wal-Mart asked us to create a cheaper entry-level stroller, we designed a "two-legged" baby carrier which cut $8 dollars off the cost but maintained our margins. The design is light, safe, stable and easily collapses for storage; it was an instant best seller.

Q: Beyond innovation and taking advantage of the economic cycle you seem to have gone one step beyond most Chinese companies. You have created your own brands, done your own marketing and set up your own distribution network. How did you do it?

A: Innovation has been the key to opening markets, but to get through the door we needed marketing and distribution.

We have been asked may times to be an original equipment manufacturer (OEM) but we have refused. We are, however, very active in original design manufacturing (ODM) work. Some time ago, we realized that the long-term interests of our company required us to always be at the leading edge of the market, where our innovation and design could command higher margins. The alternative to be at the trailing end, where your products are treated as fungible commodities and margins are thin is not a practical alternative.

By developing and producing solutions, we were able to fund our factory expansions and showcase our design and manufacturing expertise. The client decides whether to use their brand, ours or co-brand. It has allowed us to create strategic alliances with some of the world's foremost retailers which in turn solved our distribution issues and helped market our name throughout the world.

Q: Any failures?

A: Along the way we had to adapt as necessary. We were told at one point that Goodbaby did not work well as a brand in the US, we created the Geobaby brand. When we needed a brand and distribution vehicle to enter the US market, we struck a deal with COSCO, which was in the process of exiting the market, and used their distribution network and brand recognition. In Europe, when we were approached about working with a 140-year-old British company, which

supplied the high end of the market (Lady Diana), about helping them renew their product line, we accepted. Apart from the marketing advantages, it gave us our first look, from the inside, at the top end of the market. They kept their niche in the European luxury pram market (prams for over 1,000 euros). Since then, we have worked with various world brands, including Disney and Eddie Bauer.

It was initially very difficult for us as a Chinese company to deal with marketing and distribution in other countries. We like to work with agents and other partners, but we feel that our future depends on being involved with the markets directly. Our business motto in dealing with others is "no enemies, only friends". When we work with other brands, we become the value-added supplier who can help them differentiate their product line. When we work with dealers, we show them the difference our products can make to their bottom line. When we work with retailers, we are their best friend; we help them solve their problems quickly and profitably.

Q: I can not help but be impressed with you and your company's success. What part has Kunshan played in Goodbaby's success?

A: We have created a vertically integrated design, manufacture, sales and distribution network, utilizing what we have learned and the advantages Kunshan has to offer.

Some of our success is due to the cheap, skilled labor (by developed nation's standards), inexpensive land and low construction costs, modern infrastructure, excellent logistics and an excellent relationship with Kunshan. The rest is due to our collective belief that hard work and smart people can create great things. Goodbaby took a different road from other Chinese companies, but our success is quickly becoming a clear beacon of what is possible. Like many international companies we are concerned about intellectual property and we will defend our inventions, but in the end the future belongs to the next innovation and the people who create them.

Kunshan's government has always been proud and supportive of our success and when we had issues they were quickly resolved. The difference is that Kunshan's government is proactive rather than reactive. For instance, as a company whose future depends on world-class designers, we need to attract and retain world-class talent. To help us and the other tertiary industries which are now here, Kunshan is spending 5 percent of its annual budget supporting research and development facilities, including our new design center, and attracting human resources. It means that, when we recruit returned overseas Chinese students and foreign experts, the government will pay them a bonus and help with housing. Since 2001, over 41 percent of our total staff hired globally have been foreigners or former employees of large multinational companies, like P&G., 13 percent of our employees hold foreign passports and 45 of them work in China. To retain them, we support them with training and advancement opportunities based on their ability. Our proximity to Shanghai without the pollution or cost is also a factor especially for families.

Q: Any last thoughts?

I have been asked many times what makes Goodbaby different. After thinking about it, I have a way of explaining it, which I believe applies to Goodbaby and Kunshan as well. When I was young I worked on a farm. Each day I would pass a pond and notice that the ducks would often be walking around quacking loudly on the bank, until one duck jumped in, as soon as the first duck was in the water, the rest would follow. Looking at them I decided that, when I knew where I wanted to go, I would not wait for someone else to lead. This has guided my actions and seems to apply to Kunshan's government as well. At Goodbaby, we have been successful because when we saw an opportunity we jump in. Our willingness to take the risk that our designs, manufacturing capabilities and financial investment would work, earned us profits and the trust of our foreign partners. It has been the key to our position in the industry. Kunshan's government is also willing to invest and take calculated risks when the objectives are clear. They start by studying and understanding the needs of the industries, they are trying to promote, then they plan and execute swiftly. Their "inside the wall, outside the wall" approach to supporting businesses has been unique and combined with their efficient "Mashang Ban" service model has made Kunshan famous and successful.

Author's Note

I met Mr. Song at his factory. We were late and it was already after 6 pm, but he greeted us warmly and conducted the presentation in person. Throughout the interview he was enthusiastic and charming. Afterwards he took us on a tour of the factory display area, a cavernous building the size of a small department store, and gave us a tour only an inventor could give. He discussed the major innovations which had kept Goodbaby growing and his perspective on the industry and he summarized the difference in customer demands in different parts of the world. It turned into a verbal history lesson of the technical and marketing innovations, mechanisms, safety and cost issues which had defined Goodbaby and the industry.

It was a pleasure talking to Mr. Song and it was easy to understand why the company is so successful. This is a man who enjoys the process of what he is doing and does it well. He is also a man who is responsible for restructuring an industry and building its dominant player.

Goodbaby is an example of what Chinese industry could become and we should be watching carefully. For a long time, the developed world has assumed that we would retain the edge in terms of innovation. Why do we make this assumption? As market opportunities move east, so will the talent. Backed by economic development models like the Kunshan Way, China has become a formidable force which we need to understand better if we are to respond.

Compal Electronics

Interview with Mr. Robert Shyn

Mr. Robert Shyn (Taiwanese), Vice President, Compal Electronics Technology (Kunshan) Co., Ltd.

Q: Can you summarize Compal's history?

A: Established in 1984, Compal Electronics' professional management team has earned an industrywide reputation for fast, flexible, high-quality design and manufacturing. By winning the trust of its customers Compal has become one of the leading global IT companies in its industry. In 2008, total annual revenue reached US12.83 billion dollars with a worldwide workforce over 30,000. In addition to its manufacturing facilities Compal provides leading edge customer service through its worldwide network of service branches located in Brazil, U.S., Poland and China (including mainland and Taiwan).

Mr. Robert Shyn, Vice President, Compal Electronics Technology (Kunshan) Co., Ltd.

Q: Who are your clients?

A: Compal is the number one worldwide manufacturer of notebook PCs. We provide total solutions for HP, Acer, Toshiba, Dell and other global brands.

Q: What attracted you to Kunshan?

A: We first heard about Kunshan through friends in Taiwan. When we investigated we were impressed with the local government's commitment to building a comprehensive supply chain network. As an ODM, we compete by providing clients with total solutions including design, manufacturing, logistics, distribution and after-market services. Our clients prefer to concentrate on their brand image and sales. Our business model depends on keeping costs low and efficiency high. Having our suppliers nearby cuts our product development cycles down significantly, for instance, it used to take one and a half years to get some products designed and ready to go four years ago, right now the same process can be done in three months.

Q: What has Kunshan done for your company?

A: Kunshan provided us a total solution, including incentives and customized service based on our size and needs. We've been here for 10 years; our relationship with local government is very close. We understand local government and feel that they are more like a partner. Our relationship here is completely different from any government relationship we have anywhere else in the world.

Q: Whom do you stay in close contact with at the local government?

A: Because the export processing zone is important to our daily shipping and operations we are interfacing with them on a daily basis. The KETD leaders stay in contact with us and we feel we have excellent access to the city leaders if we need it. As one of leading companies in Kunshan, we interact with different parts of the government every week. In many instances it is just to exchange ideas and make sure we are aware of each other's plans. We work 335 days a year and each day we work to the "99-1" rule it adds a lot of pressure but it is how we do our business. It would be hard to imagine doing this anywhere else with the same efficiency.

Q: The Kunshan government is very interested in seeing companies like yours climb the value-added ladder, is this your plan and how do you intend to proceed?

A: We are currently building an R&D center in Kunshan and we believe that we can continue to serve our customer base with the type of solutions and service they need by creating new proprietary solutions which add to their and our bottom line.

We believe that Kunshan will become the next worldwide IT integration location for business. By being able to combine innovation and efficiency you create the perfect environment.

In today's fast-paced marketplace you have to get your solutions to market while you work on the next generations of solutions. Too many places think that research alone will carry you but implementation is half of the game. For instance in Kunshan we are able to follow the "99-1" rule: 99 percent of the days manufactured products are shipped out in one day. We believe it will be the combination of factors which will allow Kunshan to mature into a successful international integrated research/development/manufacturing center.

Q: How does Compal view China's changing role from a production base to a market opportunity?

A: One of the reasons we selected Kunshan as our main operations and future R&D center is that we think the Chinese market is as important as the US market. By building our R&D center here we will be close to our manufacture base which we believe is necessary to create the efficiencies required by fiercely competitive nature of our industry. We know that relying on our R&D center in Taiwan is too costly in terms of time, communications and money. By doing our design in the mainland we can save 30 percent in costs and cut our tooling time significantly because the designers will have direct access to the tooling suppliers who are based in Kunshan.

Q: As a margin-sensitive business you must follow low costs and efficiency or lose business to competitors who do. How will Kunshan be able to hold on to your business if costs start to increase?

A: We have some investments in Vietnam and other countries and we keep a careful eye on comparative costs. The equation will always be based on the total cost package, cheaper labor, by itself, will not make up for inadequate infrastructure, logistical issues, delays due to political risk or inefficiency. I believe Kunshan is pursuing the logical path by encouraging more research and development, actively strengthening the supplier network and providing fast efficient services. It helps that Taiwan and mainland are close and it is easier for us to understand each other.

Q: On a different note, do you enjoy living in Kunshan?

A: Yes. It's like our second hometown. The development has been step by step. Existing brands attract more brands, and new brands attract more new brands. It's kind of an upward spiral which I expect to continue as long as Kunshan's government is managing things carefully. At each step in the spiral the quality of life improves as more business creates demand for more services. I believe that our partners like Toshiba and Dell may someday build their operation center in Kunshan because of what it has to offer.

China offers us and other firms a great opportunity, young smart graduates, a growing domestic market and a rapidly improving quality of living. I have been surprised that my house in Vancouver has stayed the same while my house in

Shanghai went from 8K/square meters to 30K/square meters. It underlines in my mind that China is where the opportunities are.

Leading the pack– Kunshan New and Hi-Tech Industrial Development Zone—out of China's sixty-five provincial-level EDZs it ranked number one in terms of gross industrial output

Author's Note

With over 1,000 businesses in Kunshan the Taiwanese community has become a partner in Kunshan's future, the importance of which is exemplified in a local catchphrase, 'Five, Six, Seven, Eight, and Nine'; it describes the significance of Taiwanese involvement in Kunshan, 50 percent of fiscal revenue, 60 percent of tax, 70 percent of sales, 80 percent of investment and 90 percent of trade come from Taiwanese investment.

Compal and the other businesses which were originally just economic business refugees fleeing Taiwan's uncompetitive manufacturing environment, have since through a series of investments, informational exchanges and sheer numbers created a Taiwan-friendly economic oasis. Interestingly the local Kunshan people seem to have dispensed with the usual resentment which would generally follow such a large migration. What the future holds will depend on a number of issues which are beyond the Kunshan people or their Taiwanese guests' control. Comparative costs and exchange rates are played out in the national sandbox, but it is interesting to see both sides striving to control the things they can such as innovation, talent recruitment, supplier networks, logistics, services and access to China's growing domestic markets.

Capgemini

With more than 92,000 employees, Capgemini is a global leader in consulting, technology and outsourcing. Headquartered in Paris, Capgemini's regional operations include North America, Europe and Asia-Pacific.

Capgemini has a unique way of working with its clients, which it calls the Collaborative Business Experience. Through commitment to mutual success and the achievement of tangible value, the company helps businesses implement growth strategies and leverage technology, and thrive through the power of collaboration. With more than 92,000 employees from 36 countries on three major continents (Europe, America, and Asia-Pacific), Capgemini is ranked within the top three companies in the professional services industry.

Capgemini started its operation in China in 1997. With the rapid growth of business, China has become Capgemini's focus for business expansion in the Asia-Pacific region. Capgemini Global Delivery and Shared Service Center was established in Kunshan Huaqiao Economic Development Zone in October, 2008. As a world leading software delivery agency, this center is developing five major businesses in China: management service for application system; software design and development service; testing service for industrial software and systems; business process outsourcing; as well as IT infrastructure service. As a world leading consulting firm, Capgemini has developed new business in China, such as BPO (business process outsourcing) and IT outsourcing. Starting with 200, we plan to have 2,000 employees in the outsourcing business within three years. Our main business in Kunshan will be expanding our financial and non-financial service business which currently has 20,000 employees globally.

Capgemini Group's new Kunshan headquarters

Mr. Wang Xiaoliang (George), General Manager of Capgemini Kunshan

Interview with Mr. Wang Xiaoliang

Mr. Wang Xiaoliang (George), General Manager of Capgemini Global Delivery and Shared Service Center (Kunshan). Born in Northeast China, he grew up in Tianjin, worked five years after college (find names of schools and dates, maybe best to send him an e-mail) in China, pursued a master's in Canada, worked for Novell, then RIM in 2000 (coding work), came back to China in 2003 to work for Bearing Point as an operation manager (formerly KPMG consulting), joined Unisys as head of operation director of its global research center and then his former boss asked him to join Capgemini in 2006.

Q: What is Capgemini's China strategy?

A: Initially Capgemini China was focusing on providing services to the domestic Chinese market, but China's political stability, skilled work force and developing markets have made it an attractive part of Capgemini's global outsourcing strategy.

Q: Is language a problem especially during the process of localization?

A: Language was a problem ten years ago. Today we only need to make sure that employees who interface directly with clients, like team leaders and project managers, speak English well. The majority of our employees are on the computers everyday and their English reading and writing is more than sufficient. Actually, I have found that Chinese English accent is probably the best English spoken in Asia as it does not suffer from the localizing effects you get in Hong Kong and Singapore.

Q: Have you been able to find the human resources you need?

A: Yes, we just recruited 40 Chinese college graduates recently. Ironically, the financial service unit interviews were handled by our Indian operations. Over the long run, we are concerned and will be watching Kunshan's efforts to recruit high-value technical and management resources and expand its educational system.

Q: What drives your industry?

A: The most important issues in the outsourcing industry are costs and human resources. Costs in China are increasing, but still under control, about a third of Western countries. Currently, China and India are close; the main differences are political stability and infrastructure. Both countries have human capital and vibrant economies. But, because Capgemini is paid to deliver results it needs to manage political and infrastructure risk by having a global strategy which can allow it to adjust as needed. India's rapid rise in the outsourcing industry has driven human resource costs, and in view of current events, an eye has to be kept on political risk and physical infrastructure. China's ability to manage its domestic system and build reliable infrastructure like roads and power makes it attractive.

Q: Why did you come to Kunshan?

A: The company used an extensive search process to identify the best potential locations. In the end, after visiting Dalian, Chengdu, Suzhou, Shanghai, Tianjin and Nanjing, we chose Kunshan even though it had no outsourcing businesses.

Q: What in particular impressed you?

A: We were impressed by local government's knowledge of our industry and specific needs and proximity to Shanghai. Rather than trying to minimize issues, Kunshan presented its business plan for addressing and solving the issues we presented, which was more impressive than the usual vague "don't worry we will take care of that" assurances we got from other cities.

It also helped that Kunshan's enthusiasm was evident from the moment we arrived, and also the direct access we had to the Party secretary, mayor and every department head we needed to talk to about our requirements. Every issue and question we needed answers to from the office park master plan, affordable employee housing, discrete power supplies, transportation, licenses and occupancy permits were handled through our project manager. Our project manager was also our one point of contact with the Economic Development Zone and the Kunshan city government. So, rather than

spending our time trying to figure out the system, we were able to concentrate on setting up our business operations.

In addition to meeting with government representatives, we talked to local businesses and looked at the history. What we saw was careful strategic planning, focused implementation and consistent customer service. Bottom line, in Kunshan, we found a government which would tell us what they were going to do and then do it. When a date and price were agreed upon everything was done on time, on budget and on schedule.

Frankly, we were amazed at how quickly and smoothly things were able to proceed. In Shanghai, the permitting process alone would have taken three months. It is one of the reasons why Capgemini is moving our China headquarters from Shanghai to Kunshan. The issue comes down to service and speed; in Kunshan we can get an answer in days as opposed to months.

Q: What trends do you see developing in your industry and do they favor Kunshan?

A: More outsourcing business is moving from India to China. Even a number of Indian companies, like Tata, have set up branches in China.

China's market growth is causing a gravitational pull which is drawing in Capgemini's global clients.

The balance between sourcing from, and selling into, the Chinese market has shifted dramatically, in large part due to the financial crisis, but also in response to growing Chinese domestic demand.

The move to localize is creating incremental consequences, as companies transfer knowledge to their Chinese employees. The combination of knowledge and experience is affecting everything from Chinese culture to business start-ups.

Q: What is Kunshan's competitive advantage?

A: Kunshan, like Shanghai, is proactive. When the central government gives them the green light to open up new areas, like the financial and transportation sectors, they go after it.

Most Chinese cities tend to be less attentive and more passive. Kunshan is focused and aggressive. They learn about the sectors they are going after, they create the infrastructure necessary to support business, they are constantly looking at successful development models and they move quickly.

Q: What is your relationship with local government and what would you say to others?

A: The relationship with local government is more like a partnership. If we have an issue or a suggestion, it will get a fair and knowledgeable response. Because of these factors I would definitely recommend the area to interested businesses.

Q: Do you and your family live in Kunshan?

A: My wife and kids live in Shanghai, but I bought an apartment in Kunshan. Although it is only a 50-minute drive between the Huaqiao Economic Development Zone and my home in the Pudong District of Shanghai, the apartment is useful when the press of business requires me to work longer hours.

The other major considerations are schools and life style; having moved from Canada, my spouse and children prefer the more cosmopolitan amenities of Shanghai and the selection of schools. The cons are Shanghai traffic, air quality and the costs for housing, help and day-to-day living expenses, which can be stratospheric compared to Kunshan.

There are also other differences; the house I bought in Canada several years ago has not appreciated, while my apartment in Shanghai has tripled in value. I am fairly optimistic that my apartment in Kunshan will do equally as well in the coming years.

I think Kunshan and Shanghai are like New Jersey and New York. Shanghai, like New York, is the draw but Kunshan, like New Jersey, offers a comfortable lower-cost alternative for working and living. It also offers a much shorter route to the city hall, what would take months or years to do in Shanghai can be accomplished in days or weeks in Kunshan. It is an important factor because in China good relations with the local government are extremely important.

Q: Do you have any concerns about Kunshan?

A: Kunshan needs to continue its human resource recruitment efforts, and develop more international education facilities (my family uses an international hospital in Shanghai).

Kunshan needs to continue climbing the value chain in terms of attracting more value-added industries which rely on innovation more than mass production.

Kunshan needs to control, and as necessary, move or reject primary and secondary industries which have adverse ecological effects.

Kunshan needs to continue improving its ecology, public and entertainment amenities which will be vital to its future attractiveness as a desirable place to live.

Kunshan needs to promote itself in a focused way which can overcome the two-city issue (most foreigners are only aware of two cities in China, Beijing and Shanghai).

Author's Note

Many companies like Capgemini are using a dual-development strategy which puts offices in China and India to guard against political, pricing and currency risk. China has quickly become a must-have part of the business equation for outsourcing companies. The additional advantage of China is that, as its manufacturing, research and the domestic sales markets have grown, so have the needs for the types of back-office services we regard as commodities. For us, back-office and technical support are pieces to be purchased on the world markets at the lowest price, but in China these areas have not been developed and are seen as areas of needed domestic expertise. Outsourcing providers like Capgemini, by being in China, are able to sell their services as a commodity to the West and as expertise in China.

With the world's fastest-growing major economy, a large pool of available skilled workers, a stable political and currency environment and a rapidly evolving infrastructure, China will continue to be a major factor in the international outsourcing industry. Companies looking for stability, cost reduction, good infrastructure and low political risk have to look at China as part of the business equation. Where they choose to be within China will be driven by access to skilled value-priced human capital, reliable infrastructure, living conditions and ease of doing business.

The important thing to note is that Kunshan formulated and executed a plan to take advantage of the economic crisis to create a tertiary knowledge-based industry. While others pulled out their begging cups and wailed woe, Kunshan's leaders took a calculated risk that they could use China's national and their local advantages to attract a world leader in the outsourcing industry and they succeeded. It is not surprising that people are beginning to admire Kunshan's success, the real question is: do your local leaders have the ability and drive to do the same?

InfoVision Optoelectronics (Kunshan) Co., Ltd.

InfoVision Optoelectronics (Kunshan) Co., Ltd. (IVO) is the third 5th-generation TFT-LCD panel manufacturer in China. Its Kunshan headquarters sit on 143 hectares. The first plant occupies an area of 400 *mu*. The Jiangsu FPD Technology Academy, which is under construction, will be completed by late 2009. There are current plans to build a second- and third-phase of the plant as soon as demand ramps up.

InfoVision Optoelectronics (Kunshan) Co., Ltd.—
leading China's TFT-LCD manufacturing efforts

With a pool of returned overseas students and domestic staff, the company has patented a number of R&D technologies and developed a variety of products since it was established three years ago, including desktop displays, NB PC and LCD TV panels. It was the first plant to specialize in manufacturing panels ranging from 10.1" to 26". The firm plans to grow its business using its R&D teams to develop new product lines concentrating initially on the Chinese domestic market.

The company has stayed on course with its production schedule and became profitable in 2007. After its last production line expansion, IVO is now the largest 5th-generation TFT-LCD panel manufacturer in China.

During the financial crisis, the capacity was running at only 15 percent, the depreciation pressure was overwhelming. However, due to the Chinese government's "Home appliances going to the countryside" plan, which created the opportunity in LCD TV business, IVO quickly switched to manufacturing 26-inch LCD panels. It then developed a diversified base of clients including seven of the larger TV brands in China.

In early 2009, the product mix was: 90-percent monitors; 10-percent laptops.

By the end of 2009: 50-percent LCD TVs (26-inch), 10-percent laptops, and 40-percent monitors.

By the end of 2010: 33-percent laptops, 60-percent LCD TV's, less than 10-percent monitors.

Long-term goal: focusing on laptops which are perfect for 5th-generation Fab production products.

InfoVision Optoelectronics (Kunshan) Co., Ltd is a joint venture of Kunshan government (51 percent) and one Taiwan company (49 percent). Founded about three years ago, total investment: 1.6 billion dollars, main products: LCD panels.

Interview with Mr. Lu Boyan

Mr. Lu Boyan, born in Taiwan, went to the US for graduate school. He worked in Bell Labs and came back to Taiwan in 1995. He was later recruited by Taiwan and AU Electronics to promote LCD industry; organized four companies to invest the earliest fabrication (Fab) lines in Taiwan which started production in 1999. He worked in AU until 2006, left as executive vice president (numbers of employees in AU grew from 40 to 40,000); then joined Hon Hai Precision Industry (another Taiwan company). Mr. Lu came to work in IVO in February, 2009.

Mr. Lu Boyan, former General Manager, InfoVision Optoelectronics (Kunshan) Co., Ltd.

Q: What is IVO's market share?

A: IVO counts for 2 percent of worldwide market share, but in China, IVO is very important. There are only four 5th- generation LCD manufacturers in China: Shenzhen, Shanghai, Beijing and Kunshan. IVO is the largest but our comparative capacity is still small compared to the larger foreign manufacturers.

Q: What's your background?

A: I was previously the executive vice president of AU Electronics which counted for 18 to 20 percent of global LCD market share.

Q: How are you dealing with your larger Japanese, Taiwanese and South Korean competitors when they have more advanced technologies?

A: The fifth-generation LCD is not advanced technology (the Fab lines in Japan and South Korea have already been fully depreciated), but TFT LCD is strategically important component to China, which is looking to support domestic LCD makers, so it can claim a piece of its own consumer market. Without some assistance, it would be difficult to create a successful effort in this area. One of the issues is that the interest of loans in China is much higher than Taiwan but, on the other hand, the Taiwanese authority is very passive when it comes to promoting industries. It has been very helpful that Jiangsu Province has donated about $15 million dollars to help build IVO's display research center.

We have also been thankful for Kunshan's help in bringing customers to us, including introductions to some of largest laptop and TV makers. In addition, Kunshan government is actively helping us with supplier integration by recruiting components makers of glass, screens, IC and other key parts. One of Chinese largest TV brand KONKA has built their factory just opposite the IVO factory which will facilitate door-to-door transaction. Kunshan is also trying to get two other large domestic TV brands to locate in Kunshan as well. They have also been very active in introducing us to other potential customers like Compal Computer. I am particularly impressed with the Party Secretary who is smart, flexible and has a keen sense of business. Kunshan has been an active partner. They allow us to concentrate on our core production and innovation businesses by taking an active role in helping us with strategic link-ups and meeting new customers. Of course by helping us they are helping themselves as well, since they are a major equity owner.

Q: You seem to be in a pretty good position. What are the benefits for Kunshan?

A: In the future, if our patent filings are successful, we hope to offer China the opportunity to control key technology components which currently have to be licensed from foreign companies.

Q: What is the future of the display industry?

A: LCD fabrication is the present, OLED has potential but it is difficult to produce in large sizes, because of the complexity and cost of creating a vacuum during the manufacturing process.

Q: Why do you think Kunshan is so successful?

A: Kunshan started to bring in foreign capital early on; local leaders were smart and flexible and have learned how to deal with Taiwanese business people and the proximity to Shanghai, many of the advantages, but with lower costs.

Q: Thank you for the business insights, what's your impression of life in Kunshan?

A: Immigrant city, large Taiwanese community, convenient traffic, clean environment with much cheaper real estate and living costs than Shanghai and Taiwan. I currently have an easy balance between working in Kunshan and having some fun in Shanghai (with my wife). Actually when I eventually retire I plan to live in Shanghai.

Author's Note

Mr. Lu is one of the world's leading experts in setting up and operating Fab lines and is in the process of repeating his successes. What is noteworthy is that Kunshan is making a strategic investment on the come. The ultimate success of this calculated gamble will depend in the short run, on the Chinese government's willingness to nurse the growth of this fledgling industry, and in the long run, on developing state-of-the-art technology which can eventually be sold abroad as well as domestically. As a 51-percent shareholder it is a significant risk but the kind which could pay huge dividends. It also points to the difference between Chinese cities and their Western counterparts. Where you do see Western countries engaging in this kind of activity, rarely will you see such a direct interest at a city level.

Kunshan Visionox Display Co., Ltd.

Kunshan Visionox Display Co., Ltd.

Visionox is a high-tech enterprise integrating R&D, mass production, marketing and sales. Kunshan Visionox Display Co., Ltd. was founded in 2006, and Beijing Visionox Technology Co., Ltd. was founded in 2001. Visionox has applied and held more than 200 patents since 1998.

History:

In 1977, Organic Light Emitting Diode (OLED) materials were first discovered by Ching Tang (of Chinese origin) in Kodak Labs by accident.

In 1990s, most of the research in OLEDs was being done in Europe and USA, while the manufacturing was being done in Southeast Asia, Japan, South Korea and China (mainland and Taiwan). By 1997, the demand for displays grew steadily reaching its peak in 2000. The industry players are a small group due to the capital costs of setting up a new Fab line. There are about ten companies that are involved. Competition is brutal because it is a race to maximize your production before demand moves on to the next product line or innovation.

During the transition in the second quarter of 2006, many TFT-LCD manufacturers turned to smaller sizes, like three- to four-inch screens due to the capital costs of installing 4.5- and fifth-generation Fab lines. It immediately had an effect on the immature OLED industry; the price of small screens dropped about 50 percent in a short period of time. As a consequence, many OLED companies went bankrupt.

After the crisis, Sony successfully launched an 11-inch OLED TV in late 2007 and some South Korean companies made samples of over 30-inch OLED TV later on. Researchers and investors believed that large-size OLED TV Fab lines would be mature in three to five years. There are also Chinese companies working on this direction, some start from small-size and the others invest on the large-size products directly.

Visionox was established on the basis of Organic Light Emitting Display (OLED) technology research team of Tsinghua University, which was organized by leading Chinese OLED scientist Mr. Qiu Yong. He started to do research on OLED in 1996 and got great support from Mr. Hu Qili, former Minister of Electronics. The first Fab line was developed in Tsinghua University in 1999 and Beijing Visionox Technology Co., Ltd. was founded in 2001 to develop mass production capability. Our small-size products went to market in 2003.

In 2005, Visionox was ready for mass production and began to look for a suitable city to locate its Fab lines. Many Chinese cities were interested.

Interview with Mr. Chen Yaonan

Mr. Chen Yaonan (Charlie Chen), President, Kunshan Visionox Display Co., Ltd.

Q: Why did you choose Kunshan?

A: It has a comparatively complete electronics and display industrial supply chain. Local leaders have a good understanding and knowledge. For example, Mr. Zhu Fengquan, current Party secretary of Yushan Town and KSND, dismantled a laptop to identify necessary component makers and systematically started bringing the key manufacturers to Kunshan. Because of our connection to Tsinghua University the presence of Tsinghua's Science and Technology Park in Kunshan played an important role in assuring us about the capabilities and efficiency of the Kunshan government.

Q: How did it happen?

Mr. Charlie Chen, President, Kunshan Visionox Display Co., Ltd.

A: Visionox's original major shareholder was a Hong Kong listed company which had had a monochrome LED factory in Guangdong Province for more than 10 years. They were not very enthused about Kunshan at the beginning; however, they changed their minds after we came to Kunshan. Although we arrived at the airport at 1 am, we were greeted and taken to our hotel. 7 hours later at 8 am the vice-mayor personally showed us a number of potential sights. At 1 pm we met with the mayor (Mr. Zhang Guohua, current Party secretary) and were given a detailed presentation on the cities' understanding of our needs, including available infrastructure, industrial supply chain components suppliers who were already in Kunshan and their view of the global development market and how Kunshan planned to be part of it. Later on we learned that the presentation was put together by existing LED manufacturers with government and private industry experts. The Hong Kong shareholders were so impressed they signed a deal two hours later. Together Kunshan and the Hong Kong Company invested 120 million yuan and 280 million yuan respectively. Kunshan announced additional investment of 200 million yuan last year and has since then become our largest shareholder.

Q: What does the future hold?

A: Kunshan is developing an industrial technology research institute. Visionox and the KETD (Kunshan Economic and Technological Development Zone) are going to invest 200 million yuan and 35 million yuan respectively to build and equip the lab. Part of the institute will be devoted to a large-size flat panel display lab which we intend to use to develop the next generation of China's large-size display panels. The first Fab line will be organized and built early next year. We feel confident that with Kunshan's plan, central government support and our innovation we will be successful.

Q: You and Kunshan seem to be betting heavily on the central government's desire to capture part of the domestic display industry?

A: Yes, the Chinese central government views OLED display as one of crucial strategic industries in the future. It is listed in central government's "863 scientific development plan," and as part of both the tenth and eleventh five-year plans. Mr. Qiu Yong, Visionox's chairman and chief scientist was involved in making those plans so we feel very strongly that we understand the goals and how to achieve them. China didn't get the chance to participate in the early CRT and LCD display industries; it is determined not to let that happen in OLED technology.

Author's Note

Kunshan is betting huge amounts of resources and time to develop a Chinese display industry, but unlike their Western counterparts, if the strategy succeeds it will result in enormous direct rewards for Kunshan as well as the usual indirect benefits of having a successful hi-tech industry. There are also large possible downsides if the central government changes direction or the technology never materializes.

You can also see how private enterprises, national policies and educational institutions are put together to accomplish national goals. Again while this would not be uncommon for a nation or a large province to be doing it is not something you would expect to be planned and executed by a fifth-level city.

Motech (Suzhou) Renewable Energy Co., Ltd.

Motech Industries, Inc. (Motech) was founded in 1981, and specialized in researching of high-end test and in the design, manufacturing, marketing, and service of measuring instruments.

The company is led by Dr. Tsuo, chairman of the board and CEO. Dr. Tsuo received his Ph.D. in Physics from Yeshiva University, New York City, in 1978. He has been involved in the field of photovoltaic since 1979. Dr. Tsuo worked as a senior scientist at the National Renewable Energy Laboratory (NREL) in Golden, Colorado, the Stanford Research Institute (SRI) in Menlo Park, California, and the NASA/Langley Research Institute in Hampton, Virginia.

The company has a comprehensive list of manufacturing and quality certifications and is one of the top 10 producers of solar cells in the world. Headquartered in Taipei, it has two production facilities in Taiwan and one in Kunshan.

The Chinese subsidiary, Motech (Suzhou) Renewable Energy Co., Ltd., was founded in December, 2006, located in Kunshan New and Hi-Tech Industrial Development Zone. Construction started in March, 2007 and finished in September, 2008. It may start to make panels in 2010. Whole systems are only made in Taiwan (Motech provided the solar system on roof of Staples Arena in LA). Motech is considering vertical integration of more sophisticated process and products, but a lot depends on central government's policies (subsidies and encouraging programs).

Motech (Suzhou) Renewable Energy Co., Ltd. —One of China's leading solar energy manufacturers

Mr. Andy Pao, Vice-president, Operation Division, Motech (Suzhou) Renewable Energy Co., Ltd.

Interview with Mr. Andy Pao

Mr. Andy Pao, Vice-president, Operation Division, Motech (Suzhou) Renewable Energy Co., Ltd.

He is originally from Taiwan, he went to the US for graduate school in 1990, got married in the US and worked for an optical device company. In 2002 he moved to Shanghai to work for different optical device companies and in November, 2008 he came to Kunshan to join Motech after a six-month recruiting process.

Q: What was your initial impression of Kunshan?

A: I was impressed by how vibrant its economy was. The production scale (laptop OEMs) was surprising, given I had never heard much about Kunshan. I was also pleasantly surprised by the rapid pace of economic and technical transformation. The government had been actively recruiting new higher value-added tertiary industries like IC design, renewable energy and financial and technical outsourcing. It's creating a better business environment as it brought in a larger core of technical and business professionals.

I was also surprised at the emphasis the local government had put on social issues. The price of cheap land, labor and government project managers seemed to be a responsibility to take care of and train local employees. This was a trade-off we were more than happy to make given that it's a win-win situation. Our company work required precision manufacturing within a tightly controlled manufacturing environment, so our employees had to be trained to the highest technical levels.

Q: What factors did you look at when you were being recruited to come to Kunshan?

A: My wife and I took seven months to make the decision. We came and looked around on our own time on a number of occasions. My wife was an investment banker was concerned about a number of issues from employment to day-to-day living amenities. We liked the fact that we could get from our house in Shanghai to Kunshan by car in about one and a half hours. It gave us the sense that friends and familiar places were close enough to visit on the weekends if we wanted. We were very impressed by the size of the Taiwanese community. Being from Taiwan, it was like going to a small version of Taipei. Taiwanese people, food, culture, and even brands were everywhere, including my favorite coffee bar, "85°C", the Taiwanese version of Starbucks.

The price of housing was a big relief as it was about one third of the cost in Shanghai for a similar level of amenities. I ended up buying a house about a 20-minute drive from the factory. It is an easy commute and gives me time to make the transition between home and work. Schools were and are a big issue. We have young children; so far we are happy with the pre and primary schools near our home. We do have concerns about high school. If the local schools are not acceptable, we will send our children to boarding schools in Shanghai. We are hoping that when the time comes the options in Kunshan will be more attractive.

Another major issue is that we are Christians and we want our children to learn our values. I study the Bible on a daily basis and our spiritual life is just as important as our material one. We are happy to find a number of Taiwanese churches here and people who share our values. We have also found that the general community is curious but accepting our beliefs. As we prefer a simple family life, Kunshan's pace is more than acceptable, although others tell me there are many entertainment options available.

Q: How does your life in Kunshan differ from Shanghai?

A: In comparison with our former life in Shanghai, it is very comfortable. We were surprised to find a brand new Taiwanese hospital in Kunshan, donated as a charity project. It is even better equipped and run than most of the large hospitals in Shanghai. In addition, there are a number of Taiwanese clinics, staffed by Taiwanese trained doctors in Kunshan, which are not permitted in Shanghai.

Housing is very reasonable and the government offers housing subsidies to those who qualify under their technical and professional recruitment program. On the weekends, our family spends a lot of time in the city parks, which are free. They provide us with a quality family experience and plenty of fresh air. We certainly do not miss Shanghai's traffic and air pollution and believe we made the right choice for our children's health.

Q: Describe the relationship you have with Kunshan's government and how it differs from other places you have been in.

A: Things in Kunshan are very straightforward. The standards they expect in terms of employees and the environment are clear. We have had no problem or delays getting licenses or answers. In part, I feel this is due to the size and type of industry we represent. Environmental issues are probably the highest concern because although we make an alternative energy source which will last for 25 years, the production process has an environmental impact in terms of water and pollution. We are well aware of the local government's push for water conservation and pollution reduction, so we are constantly reviewing our options in these regards.

Q: What are the main differences between Kunshan and other places you have worked?

A: In terms of the difference between Kunshan and other places, it took less than one year to do in Kunshan what would have taken two years in Shanghai and three years in Taiwan. For the type of industry we are in, the need to get up and run quickly is essential. Capital costs are huge and product lines can be marginalized by new advancements very quickly. Kunshan's government is not only fast, it anticipates our needs. They were asking me about expansion even before I had gotten it approved by corporate.

The attention they pay to physical and human infrastructure is also impressive. Their efforts to improve the business and living environment show a long-term commitment which is often lacking, even in developed countries. In other areas I have been to, you often run into layered bureaucracies which consume time and resources and seem to get very little done.

Author's Note

As a key technical operations manager, Andy represents the kind of expertise Kunshan needs to recruit to attract and keep the kind of tertiary high value-added industries. Clearly Kunshan has a leg up on recruiting Taiwanese companies and employees. Its focus on Taiwan early on is now paying handsome dividends. But, in order to move to the next stage they will need to broaden their scope.

Andy's decision to move his family to Kunshan was based on quality of life issues which could not be found in Shanghai. If China's urban centers follow Western development patterns, it is probable that Kunshan will become a high-value living alternative to downtown Shanghai. The main piece which is in question seems to be a selection of high-quality high schools which can cater to the expectations of people from abroad.

In terms of Kunshan's efforts, you can see it is part of a recurring theme: understanding the opportunity, thorough planning, quick focused action, anticipating needs and clear lines of communication, which have created a brand of economic development which is more than extraordinary. On the other side of the equation, if the city is not interested or does not want the type of business you want to bring in, these factors would be a stiff impediment. Keep in mind that Kunshan is not just looking at opportunities randomly. Attracting large-scale renewable energy businesses, like Kunshan's push in the OLED industry, is a national priority item which the central government has been pushing for years. Kunshan is therefore following national directives, but supposedly so is every other city in China, the difference being that Kunshan has developed the tools to deliver.

Q-Technology Co., Ltd.

Q-Technology Co., Ltd. (Q-Tech) is a wholly foreign-owned enterprise (WOFE) founded in June 2007. With its initial capital being 30 million U.S. dollars, the company headquarters and production facility are located in Kunshan New and Hi-Tech Industrial Development Zone. The operational 50,000-square-meter facility which cost 55 million U.S. dollars sits on a 72,000-square-meter lot.

Q-Tech provides prepackaged electronic solutions to the electronics industry. Its global partners include Bird Sagem, VB, CKT and Lenovo. Its two main offerings are a single chip packaging and testing line which uses a proprietary mounting process to reduce cost and errors, and a packaged image sensor Compact Camera Module (CCM). The CCM line uses equipment from SUSS MicroTec, a 200mm mask and bond aligner, spin and spray coaters and wafer bond system which allows them to produce a CCM which is small, inexpensive and suitable for use in cell phones, notebook/net-book computers and the security industry.

While Q-Tech has an established business, its future lies in its ability to develop new technologies and processes. In addition to 3D chip packaging, the company plans to get into MEMS (Micro Electro-Mechanical Systems). The assumption is that there will be a continuous need for the technology and processes which allow electronics to continue shrinking, and a desire to have the solutions prepackaged and tested before they are installed in the final product. As a production facility whose future depends on developing new ideas, human capital is a priority. As a start-up, it needed to get moving quickly.

In Kunshan, it took eight months from the moment the land was bought to the time production began. In between they built a customized 50,000-square-meter facility which included space for future lines. This allowed them to cut their capital burden substantially and deliver their solutions to a market which waits for no one. The human capital equation so far has been satisfactory. Q-Tech's technical team averages four years of experience and they seem satisfied with the lower living costs yet easy access to Shanghai. They are encouraged by the fact that Kunshan is putting so much effort into attracting and retaining high-value human resources.

Interview with Mr. Zhou Hao, General Manager, Q-Technology Co., Ltd.

Q: What's your background?

A: I am a returned overseas Chinese student. I received my PhD in the US and worked in Silicon Valley and Southern California for over 10 years.

Q: Why did you choose Kunshan?

A: I chose Kunshan because I needed to keep my costs low and still be able to attract and retain high-quality talent. Kunshan's geographic location close to Shanghai, excellent access to airports and affordable and pleasant living environment made it the best place to be. I initially looked at Shanghai, it was attractive in terms of attracting human resources, but costs and bureaucracy were a major issue. I also considered Beijing but felt it was too far from the electronics markets in southern China and Taiwan. Shenzhen was also on the radar but the negatives were similar to Shanghai's. In the end, Kunshan's reputation for service and efficiency was the deciding factor.

Q: You mentioned a fast timeline, can you be more specific?

A: In November we bought the land; in December we started construction; in May construction was completed; in June the production machinery was installed and in July the production lines went into operation.

Throughout the process I had one point of contact, my government-assigned project manager who kept everything on schedule, within budget and to specification. The building was actually completed ahead of schedule and was waiting for the machinery to arrive. There is no way I could have done this in less than two years in the US. Kunshan kept every promise—utilities, water supply, power and sewer systems were sized and installed to spec with no issues or time spent on our side.

My sense of government is that they are like wolves at the door, but in Kunshan other than asking us if there is anything we need they never bother us. In most of the areas I looked at, and have been to, I have always felt more like a fat sheep that the government was eyeing up for a meal.

Q: What does the future hold for Q-Tech in Kunshan?

A: On the positive side, since coming here we have been impressed by the number and concentration of high-tech companies and we hope that there will be some profitable synergies we can take advantage of. With one half of the world's laptops being produced here, we are looking at how we can sell our solutions to the major local players.

On the negative side, the human resources are not as good as in Suzhou or Shanghai, and the laptop industry is a brutal low-margin business. We are waiting to see if the local government is able to change the mix from low margin/hi-tech to high margin/hi-tech. Product cycles move so quickly, today's innovation is next year's commodity. The only answer is to stay on the expanding edge and deliver one generation of solutions as you are developing the next. I am encouraged by the government's human resource bonus plan which is aimed at innovators and high-skilled technical people. In time as Shanghai grows out and embraces Kunshan, it will probably be easier.

One other major issue is the business outlook of investors in China which tends to be very focused on immediate opportunities rather than long-term process development. In time I hope investors realize that a good team that can produce solutions is the asset, not a couple of patents, which will be commoditized or worked around in a few years. Although this has nothing to do with Kunshan, it will have an effect on China's long-term development. On a different note I am becoming increasingly concerned about the housing and living costs in Shanghai which seem unsustainable.

Overall I am very happy with Kunshan and looking forward to the future especially if someone can point me to somebody who needs some prepackaged pre-tested solutions.

Author's Note

Dr. Zhou is the kind of entrepreneur every city is looking for. Smart, experienced and driven, he represents a new phenomenon in China—the returned Chinese. Having got their education and working experience in the West, they face massive culture shock when they return to a country they do not recognize. Physically, psychologically and linguistically, the landscape has completely changed. On top of this, the returned generation is not always welcome; those who stayed behind have no desire to share with those who left for the comforts and opportunities of the West. But the Chinese central government is anxious to mine this source of human capital. If China is going to continue its economic progress, the government knows it needs technology, process knowledge and the type of investment outlook which can create the next phase. Kunshan's human resource recruitment policies are part of the central government's directives, but the success of this effort will depend on Kunshan. It is a poignant example of how China's economic engine works.

Sinyih Ceramic

Sinyih Ceramic is a subsidiary of Taiwan Championship Construction, which is the leading provider of ceramic tiles in Taiwan. In 1997, Sinyih Ceramic was looking to locate a production facility in China mainland. The investment of 30 million US dollars represented their first investment on the mainland.

An interview with Mr. Chen Zhengsheng, General Manager of Sinyih Ceramic (China) Corporation (November, 2000)

Mr. Chen visited more than 10 EDZs in China before choosing Kunshan. As a practical businessman he was not impressed by "no problem" approach he got from most of the EDZs. He thought it odd that a group who seemed to know nothing about his business needs were so willing to assure him that there would be "no problem". Based on his business experience and understanding of human nature, he was sure that empty assurances, uttered in hopes of getting his investment, would turn into big problems later. In Kunshan, the approach was completely different, they never said "no problem," they wanted a list of our business requirements and issues and then proposed solutions which addressed them. He was impressed with the practical, workman-like approach to each issue which often involved negotiated trade-offs. In the end, he was able to approve a deal which dealt specifically with his needs. The location, in terms of its access to ports, and the word of mouth endorsements he got from other Taiwanese businessmen sealed the deal. Kunshan kept its part of the bargain and the startup was handled smoothly. When issues came up they were dealt with quickly in a way which shared unexpected costs. Today Sinyih is still in Kunshan, generating profits at a higher rate than its production facilities in Taiwan.

Author's Note

It is doubtful that Kunshan would be as interested today as it was in 1997 in this type of industry. Although Sinyih created a modern tile factory these types of factories use a significant amount of water and have environmental side effects. The interview shows how consistent Kunshan has been in its business approach. Thirteen years in China represents two to three generations of leadership. Keeping a consistent focused approach in the midst of change is an indication of an established corporate culture.

Giant Bicycle

2009 – Giant moves its headquarters and a 300-million-USD carbon fiber research facility to Kunshan

2007 – Giant becomes the world's largest quality cycle manufacturer

2006 – Giant enters the European accessories market, pumps, clothing and luggage

2002 – Giant manufactures 4,730,000 bicycles in a single year

1998 – Giant manufactures 2,840,000 bicycles in a single year

1998 – Company acquires 30 percent share of Hodaka, Japan

1997 – Chuansin Metal Products (Kunshan) Co., Ltd., China established

1996 – European Factory in the Netherlands established

1994 – Company goes public on Taiwan Stock Exchange (TWSE: 9921)

1992 – Giant Co., Ltd., China established, a production facility (29 million US dollars) is set up in the Kunshan Economic and Technological Development Zone

1991 – Giant Bicycle PTY Ltd., Australia established

1991 – Giant Bicycle Co., Canada, Inc. established

1989 – Giant Company Ltd., Japan established

1987 – Giant Bicycle Inc., USA established

1986 – Giant Europe BV, Netherlands established

1981 – Giant Sales Company, Taiwan established

1980 – Giant becomes Taiwan's largest bicycle manufacturer

1972 – Giant Manufacturing Co., Ltd., established in Taiwan

Excerpts from an interview with Liu Bing, the assistant to the General Manager of Giant Bicycle China (November, 2000)

Q: How did you end up in Kunshan?

A: We were originally looking to invest in a southern city in the mainland of China, but after a year of fruitless negotiations, a friend suggested that we look at Kunshan. When we came, we were personally greeted by the top leaders from all the departments we would need to deal with. Our greeting was "If you can give us a list of what you require, we will get you the answers". Within one week we were given a complete plan and a proposed deal. Our Taiwanese Chairman, Mr. Liu Jinbiao, could not believe it and made a personal trip to see the Governor of Jiangsu. His question was if Kunshan could

and would live up to the agreement, the Governor answered "yes".

Q: There is an interesting story about the name of the street your factory in Kunshan is located on, would you be willing to share it?

A: To be candid, while local beneficial policies are nice, there are other considerations which speak to the nature of a relationship that is just as important. The road in front of our Taiwanese factory is called Shun Fan Road. There was a strong feeling that it would be very propitious (lucky) to have the road in front of our Kunshan facility renamed to Shun Fan Road. The Kunshan government agreed immediately, even though this was a difficult request. Today our Kunshan address is No.1 Shun Fan Road. The business has gone extremely well. In combination with our factories in China's Taiwan and Europe our annual output increased from 150,000 bikes (1994) to over 2.1 million in 2000. This was an important first step in the formation of an excellent relationship with Kunshan.

Author's Note

This is a great snap shot of how Kunshan has been able to react quickly when opportunities presented themselves. It is hardly surprising that five years later, in 1997, Sinyih Ceramic was getting excellent word of mouth endorsements from their friends in Taiwan. By concentrating on an area of opportunity, like Taiwan, Kunshan built brand credibility. At the time Taiwanese companies, whether competing as OEMs or through their brands, were locked in a life-and-death struggle to reduce costs. Competitive pressures, the desire to increase the bottom line, the proximity of cheap Chinese labor and lower manufacturing costs created a powerful attraction.

Shortly after Giant set up shops in Kunshan, Shimano, a Japanese company, set up a 30-million-USD factory. Today over 10 bicycle and bicycle component makers are located in Kunshan, which is now the center of a 2-billion-USD-per-year industry.

Interview with Mr. Liu Wanfeng (Tsinghua Science Park), Vice President, Tuspark Co., Ltd., President, Tuspark (Kunshan) Co., Ltd.

Q: What is Tuspark?

A: Tuspark was founded in 1994, to be a bridge between university and business. Its role is to help to turn ideas developed in academia into products. In 2007, the overall R&D investment in all of China was 200 billion yuan, R&D investment in Tuspark: 3 billion yuan, over 1.5 percent of national sum. Tuspark in Beijing has 690,000 square meters, over 400 companies, including large corporations like Microsoft, Google, NEC (20 NASDAQ listed companies) and more than 300 SMEs.

Mr. Liu Wanfeng, President, Tuspark (Kunshan) Co., Ltd.

Q: Tuspark has become famous as a branded technology service provider, what accomplishments would you point to as being representative of the Tuspark approach?

A: After 15 years (1994-2009), over 20 of our Tuspark companies have gone public in China or on NASDAQ. Many of them were founded by teachers and students in China and returned overseas students. There are over 800 Tusparks in different cities throughout China which are managed and in some cases funded by Tsinghua University. Tuspark in Kunshan has the distinction of being the only park in which Tsinghua University holds the majority of shares.

Jiangsu Skyray Instrument Co., Ltd.,—Tsinghua Science Park, Kunshan—spectroscopy, chromatography and mass spectrum analytical and testing instrument manufacturing

Q: What is Tuspark doing in Kunshan?

A: Tuspark in Kunshan has one district (office zone) and two parks (industrial manufacture base and biotech base) located on 2,460 acres. Our overall development and construction plan will be finished by 2011. By then we will have another 2,000 acres ready for development.

Kunshan was selected 6 years ago, from among a number of Yangtze River Delta candidates. It was selected based on its location, mature industrial base and the quality of the local government leadership. Kunshan's location of being close to Shanghai is important, hi-tech companies are cost-sensitive but also need to be close to major cities. Kunshan industrial base is at a stage where it can support new product development and manufacturing. The caliber of Kunshan's leaders is impressive. They have excellent operational capabilities; they understand our business model; they know what it takes to develop domestic and international businesses and industries and they are forward thinking. I particularly liked their idea to change "Made in Kunshan" to "Created in Kunshan". Kunshan also appealed to me and others at Tsinghua University because it had a long and rich cultural history which we believe is the X element in creating a creative new-tech cluster.

Q: Who are your clients in Kunshan Tuspark?

A: At present, we have over 70 hi-tech companies in Tuspark Kunshan; at least three companies will go public in the next two years. Examples include: the first OLED Fab line in China (Visionox) and Skyray Instrument Co., Ltd., the world's leading high-technology enterprise specializing in the development, manufacture and sales of analytical and testing instruments in spectrum, chromatograph and MS fields.

Q: What kind of service do you provide?

A: We provide space which although limited can in our opinion provide the makings of dreams. Whatever you need from hardware to software, from physical to intangible services we will try to provide. These include incubation services for developing enterprises: everything from helping entrepreneurs develop their business plan, to assisting them to obtain capital, file patents, license technology and obtain and train staff and technicians. We can also provide equipment, access to VC and Angel funding (mainly centered on manufacturing and biotech currently).

Q: What areas of biotech are being developed in Kunshan?

A: Mostly research and production of RNA (nucleic acid, liquid synthesizing)

Q: What new areas are you looking at?

A: New enterprises include a business incubator for foreign SMEs and providing training and human resources service support for large multinational companies that are interested in building R&D facilities in Tuspark.

Q: Why do you have so many different development zones in Kunshan?

A: Different development zones are aimed at different clients, companies and industries. Each zone or park is just like one flower in the large garden of Kunshan. Our theory is based on what Finland does. A small country it leads the world in per capita R&D investment. It has over 1,000 science parks and it fuels its economy with new ideas and products developed in them. As China starts to close the IP gap it needs more science parks which can help to create the solutions we and

the world need. In so doing we will also change the Chinese economic structure.

Q: How is life in Kunshan? (Mr. Liu's wife and kid live in Beijing)

A: I started living and working in Kunshan six years ago, and have been very impressed by the infrastructure improvements and the ambition and perspective of the people. For me life is easy, quiet and comfortable. Fishing is great, but entertainment options like music concerts, theatre and art shows are limited. Kunshan's soft environment has not kept pace with its economy, but I am encouraged by the Kunshan government efforts to build new concert and entertainment venues. I believe that when we have the new research and development facilities set up there will be an increased demand for a greater variety of entertainment options. Kunshan has a long history of advanced culture and it will blossom again as time goes on.

Author's Note

Tuspark is a good idea but its success will depend on the people it can attract and the quality of services it can offer. The part of the park I visited was modern and beautifully laid out. It reminded me of a Silicon Valley corporate tech campus.

One area where Tsinghua could be helpful would be if it were willing to set up a satellite campus offering postgraduate studies in the areas Kunshan is trying to grow. Although Kunshan has attracted a great number of educational institutions over the last 5 years, having a postgraduate program run by Tsinghua University would give the area some academic heft and be a conduit for graduates to find useful areas of study and jobs.

Week Nine Ecology Village

Week Nine, in the western part of Kunshan, sits on about 700 acres. It has been designated as a demonstration site for National Agricultural Tourism which is a designation given to promote tourism as a means of helping the economies of rural areas. It has an orchard, mini zoo, vegetable greenhouse, garden, tea house/coffee bar, a number of eating areas, a barbeque area and a fishing pond where you catch fish and they will cook them.

The village is an agricultural tourist park with a variety of family-oriented activities aimed at locals, day trippers and tourists. The emphasis is on providing a relaxing way to spend a morning or afternoon eating healthy food and learning about agriculture. The main attractions are the rows of hot houses which double as agricultural showcases for different varieties of plants and animals. From a functional point of view, it also allows those interested, to see and taste the different agricultural products. The park is then able to assist those interested in sourcing or growing these new varieties.

This being China a big part of the experience is having lunch or dinner at one of the many eating areas on the grounds. Organic meats and produce grown on site are the specialties of the house. For the children there is children's play area and day camp facility, which caters to urban families looking to get their kids away from polluted air, noise, endless studying and video games. Although there are a number of these parks around Kunshan, they are still trying to refine the business model in terms of product and profitability.

Interview with Mr. Wu Niandu

Mr. Wu, Vice President of Week Nine Ecology Village, met us in the teahouse and then gave us a frenetic tour of the grounds in an oversized golf cart. Originally from Taiwan, he had previously retired after a career running factories in Guangdong. He was talked out of retirement six months ago, to help with the direction and operation of the park, by his friend and senior colleague, Wang Jiuquan, President of Week Nine Ecology Village. Wang had started the venture in 2003, partly as a hobby and partly out of his desire to promote friendly relations with Kunshan. Mr. Wu was full of enthusiasm about the expansion plans for the park and talked at great length about the future of the business.

Q: What's your plan for the future of this village?

A: The plan is to introduce some Taiwanese and some foreign plants, fruits and agricultural technologies to Kunshan, build a following for organic foods from our restaurants and create an educational experience for kids to learn and appreciate the natural environment.

Q: Why was this ecological village started?

A: It was started seven years ago for fun, by my friend and senior colleague Wang Jiuquan, President of Week Nine Ecology Village, as a retirement hobby and means of sharing agricultural knowledge, opportunities and friendship. Kunshan has been very hospitable to the people from Taiwan and this is one way the friendship can be reciprocated. We have been losing money but our hope is to refine the model and then promote it on a larger scale.

Q: In the US, people in large cities are the ones who accept "organic" idea first. Farmers generally don't care. Is it the same here?

A: Yes. More and more Chinese people, especially rich people have been aware of the advantages of organic products. It'll take some time for farmers to believe and accept that. The mainland has developed very quickly, sometimes even too quickly. Social and consumer development has not developed as quickly as the economy. I think things will slow down a little bit and concepts like this ecology village will catch on.

Q: Coming from Taiwan, how do you like Kunshan?

A: I feel like I am in my second home. There are no language problems, many friends and a wonderful selection of Taiwanese restaurants and snack food places. The local people are friendly and open and the government is very supportive of our efforts.

Q: Do you mind if I ask you questions related to Taiwan?

A: No problem.

Q: How did Kunshan become attractive to Taiwan businessmen, even though Guangdong was open much earlier and is much closer?

A: Fifteen years ago, the Pearl River Delta was more attractive to Taiwanese businessmen because of its geographic location. Hong Kong's port facilities were a crucial link to Taiwan manufacturers. Kunshan was extremely proactive in going after Taiwanese business at a time when Taiwan's businesses were under competitive pressure to cut costs. Kunshan's ability to make strategic deals quickly and follow through on their promises created an excellent word of mouth reputation which circulated among our business people. While Guangdong was convenient it was more complicated.

Q: Given your manufacturing background, what effect do you think the financial crisis will have on Kunshan? Will it affect the Taiwanese OEMs?

A: Both answers depend on the same issues. Kunshan was not badly affected by the financial crisis because the main businesses here are electronic factories, not clothing or shoe factories. A lot will depend on how effective Kunshan is in attracting new high-value firms and encouraging its existing OEMs to climb the value-added chain. Many OEMs here are concerned about the increasing labor costs. All depends on each entrepreneur's strategy and decision.

Author's Note

Kunshan success has attracted numerous business concepts, it remains to be seen which ones will do better than others, but if all else fails, the land which the ecology park sits on will eventually be worth a fortune as the city develops.

What It All Means

As you can see, the success of the Kunshan Way is based not only on its planning and service philosophy, but on China's central-planning-local-implementation structure and the commitment of its people. Ironically, what at first glance appears to be a very restrictive economic system has enabled local cities to be far more creative and proactive than their Western counterparts. To create and sustain its success Kunshan studied, and continues to study, successful cities from around the world and adapt their ideas to its local conditions. The success of the system is apparent in the results it has created.

Today Kunshan continues to take calculated risks based on central government directives. Its investments in targeted hi-tech optical display, new energy and research centers are examples of a new type of working relationship between government and business. The success of its model is something cities from around the world should study and adapt to their needs. It is clear that industries and companies will be considering these factors as they weigh where and what they intend to do.

SIEMENS

鴻海®

DENSO

TOSHIBA

ASHLAND

HITACHI

tyco

Chevron

TOTAL

 BOC

SUNTORY

POSCO

 Tetra Pak

统一企业®

Some of Kunshan's domestic and international corporate citizens

Investment Policies

Taxation Policy

The newly-revised Enterprise Income Tax Law of the People's Republic of China came into force in January 1, 2008. In accordance with the law, the rate of enterprises was set at 25 percent for all foreign and domestic companies. There were, however, a number of provisions which apply to SMEs and key hi-tech companies.

Small-scale enterprises with minimal profits, that qualify, pay 20 percent reduction.

High and new technology enterprises that require key state support are subject to a 15-percent tax rate. In addition, weighted deductions may be used against taxable income for research and development fees incurred by enterprises in the development of new technology, new products and new skills. The investment by enterprises on procurement of special facilities for environmental protection, energy and water conservation and safe production may be subject to an offset tax amount at a certain ratio. Enterprises set up with approval prior to the promulgation of this law that enjoy low preferential tax rates of 15 percent and 24 percent in accordance with the tax laws and administrative regulations at the current period may gradually transit to the new tax rate over a period of five years after the implementation of the law. Where such enterprises were enjoying regular tax exemptions and reductions, the treatment continues to apply until expiry after the implementation of the law. However, those entities which have shown no profits prior to the date of the implementation of the new laws will be entitled to calculate and use their deductions from the year this law is implemented.

Land Policy

There are three formulas for acquiring land: direct transfer or leasing of state-owned land or open market transfers of existing land rights.

Human Resource Policy

Kunshan is spending 100 million yuan every year to attract and cultivate creative and talented technicians and professionals. In addition, the city will provide investment programs and start-up capital for those who start businesses in Kunshan. Direct subsidies are provided as incentives to attract qualified personnel, including cash incentives and housing subsidies.

Export Processing Zone Policies

The zone practices a policy of "inside the territory while outside the customs," which includes "Four No's," "Four Exemptions," "Complete Bond" and "One Rebate."

"Four No's" means:
1. No deposit account system;
2. No registration requirement;
3. No VAT or consumption tax on products processed in the zone; and
4. No export quotas or license management for products going in and out of the zone.

"Four Exemptions" are:
1. No tax on imported machines, equipment, modules or parts used for production or maintaining equipment in the zone;
2. No tax on machines, equipment or materials needed for infrastructure or constructing plants or warehouses;
3. No tax on certain amount of office supplies for enterprises and administrative institutions in the zone; and
4. No export tariffs on finished products, leftover materials, sample products, defective goods or waste products created within the zone.

"Complete Bond" means complete bonding service for raw materials, parts, components, packaging materials and consumables that are imported to be used in the manufacturing or processing of products.

"One Rebate" means that goods going into the zone are counted as exports and qualify for rebates.

The Kunshan Export Processing Zone is among the first to create a program that allows goods to be transferred further outside the physical zone without losing their exempt status if they are then exported.

Investment Procedures

Examination and Approval Procedures for the Establishment of a Sino-foreign Joint Venture or Sino-foreign Cooperation Enterprise in Kunshan

Foreign investor

Sign letter of intent between Chinese and foreign sides

Submit a program feasibility study report to Kunshan Bureau of Foreign Trade and Economic Cooperation, Kunshan Development and Reform Commission, Kunshan Trade and Economic Committee or the Administrative Committee of Kunshan Economic and Technological Development Zone

Submit the enterprise charter to Kunshan Bureau of Foreign Trade and Economic Cooperation, Kunshan Development and Reform Commission, Kunshan Trade and Economic Committee or the Administrative Committee of Kunshan Economic and Technological Development Zone

Initial application at Kunshan Bureau for Industry and Commerce for a name of the enterprise

Submit an environment protection application to Kunshan Bureau of Environment Protection

Sign a letter of agreement on land uses with Kunshan Bureau of Land and Resources

Apply for an approval certificate from Kunshan Bureau of Foreign Trade and Economic Cooperation or the Administrative Committee of Kunshan Economic and Technological Development Zone

The approving authority issues an approval certificate

The enterprise registers at Kunshan Bureau for Industry and Commerce and receives business license within one month

The enterprise is thereby established

Examination and Approval Procedures for the Establishment of a Wholly Foreign-funded Enterprise in Kunshan

Foreign investor

Submit an application form for the establishment of a wholly foreign-funded enterprise in China with a written feasibility study report

Initial application at Kunshan Bureau for Industry and Commerce for a name of the enterprise

Submit an environment protection application to Kunshan Bureau of Environment Protection

Sign a letter of intent on land uses with Kunshan Bureau of Land and Resources

Apply for an approval certificate from Kunshan Bureau of Foreign Trade and Economic Cooperation or the Administrative Committee of Kunshan Economic and Technology Development Zone

The approving authority issues an approval certificate

The enterprise registers at Kunshan Bureau for Industry and Commerce and receives business license within one month

The enterprise is thereby established

New Foreign Investment Registration Procedures (case study example)

The following is a check sheet of procedures and timeline for the registration of a dental material manufacturing plant which was set up in Kunshan. It gives you an idea of the steps and time it takes to set up a company in Kunshan.

Kunshan XXX Dental Care Materials Co., Ltd., New Investment Registration

Name		Kunshan XXX Dental Care Materials Co., Ltd.	Issue	Establishment (leased factory)
Content	Investment scale	Registered capital: 80 M yuan; Total committed investment: 114.2 M yuan		
	Business description	Manufacture, sales and import/export of dental care materials		
Officer	Date	Procedures		
	2009-3-10	Corporate name registration (Foreign Investment window of the Bureau for Industry and Commerce's division within Administrative Approval Service Center)		
	2009-3-12	Name registered. Environmental issues approval (Environment Office in related development zone)		
	2009-3-13	Environmental issues approval (Environment Office in related district); Environmental reports sent to Environment window of Environmental Protection Bureau's division within Administrative Approval Service Center		
	2009-4-2	Environmental reports approved (environmental assessment report completed)		
	2009-4-2	Registration at Foreign Trade & Economic Cooperation Bureau		
	2009-4-2	Registration at Technology Supervision Bureau		
	2009-4-2	Approval Certificate issued by Foreign Trade & Economic Cooperation Bureau		
	2009-4-3	Materials sent to the Bureau for Industry and Commerce		
	2009-4-3	Materials sent to Foreign Investment window of the Bureau for Industry and Commerce's division within Administrative Approval Service Center		
	2009-4-8	Business License issued by the Bureau for Industry and Commerce		
	2009-4-8	Chop making and registration at Police Station		
	2009-4-9	Chop completed and application for Corporate Code Certificate submitted		
	2009-4-10	Corporate Code Certificate completed and registered at Taxation Bureau		
	2009-4-10	Taxation issues registered, official corporate bank account opened, registration with State Administration of Foreign Exchange		
	2009-4-17	Registration at customs		
	2009-4-30	Registered at customs		

The case study above is provided by Foreign Trade & Economic Cooperation Bureau of Kunshan.

Chapter 5
Kunshan's Future

To talk about Kunshan's future is impossible unless you understand what Kunshan is, to understand what Kunshan is, you must understand its relationship to China's central government and the people and energy which are part of the Kunshan Way.

As part of this it is important to appreciate Kunshan's novel urban development approach, which works within China's unique central-policy-local-implementation system. An approach which has created a new Chinese economic development model that challenges traditional Western notions; notions that strong central government controls are incompatible with capitalistic free markets. In fact China's

View of Kunshan from Tinglin Mountain

success brings into question whether, in some instances, strong central government systems are better suited to controlling the vagaries of capitalist free market systems especially during times of growth and crisis. I am not suggesting that this is suitable for all countries, but given the relative newness of our modern ideological notions and the differences in cultures and circumstances; it would be more, rather than less, probable that there are and will be different and evolving solutions to man's social organization.

Unfortunately, little attention has been paid to how China and cities like Kunshan have accomplished their economic miracle. In part this is due to the working realities of China's economic engine, which involves substantially different cultural, social, economic and political assumptions that many in the West are not familiar with.

Culturally it is hard for people in the West to grasp that the relationship between individuals and society can be so fundamentally different from Western norms. Socially and economically, we find it even more difficult to understand China's development model, which reverses Western approaches to the "horse and cart" relationship between "market" and "policy". In China "social policy", not the "market mechanism", is the "horse" that pulls the cart. Politically it is also difficult for us to understand China's unique mix of pragmatic "market" policies and Communist ideology and what it means domestically and internationally.

The issues referenced in the first chapter, ignorance of China's ancient and modern history; the self-serving views of modern day economic buccaneers; the popularized conspiracy theorists and China's silence are both the causes and symptoms

of the fundamental misunderstanding between East and West.

It does not help that the media, both foreign and domestic, expresses China's progress in fiscal rather than social measurers. The constant use of terms like GDP, FDI, trade surplus, etc... obscures China's social goals and achievements. It confuses many into believing that China has adopted some form of capitalist communism as an ideology. To the contrary the government seems less interested in ideology than pragmatic policies that improve the lives of its citizens and justifies the Party's administrative role. This is not to suggest that China's continued rise will follow the same direction, but to date China has concentrated on searching externally for ways to deal with internal issues.

What does this have to do with Kunshan's future? It's difficult to project what will happen, until you understand what has happened. Kunshan future depends on its ability to exist within a system of central government directives. You therefore can not understand Kunshan's future without understanding China's future, which is why there has been so much discussion about the direction of China. Within this framework Kunshan's main advantages are its location and the ability of its people to implement initiatives based on government policies better than their sibling rival cities. Given that its proximity to Shanghai will not change, the main variable will be the decisions and actions of its leaders and people. Its advantage is its strong historical and corporate culture, which supports innovation and action. The difficulty is that to keep its standing as China's number one county-level-city there can be no room for complacency as Kunshan faces fierce competition domestically and internationally.

The point of offering you the views of the government officials, business leaders and ordinary people was to give you a sense from those who created and live in

On the right:
Yangcheng Lake, where the famous crabs come from

Looking down on the sports center from the forest park

Taking a stroll along the Lou River

the city what their understanding, direction and roles are and how things were accomplished in the past. Like an iceberg, what is seen is only part of the reality. The daily litany of numbers used to express China's economic success, not only obscure China's social agenda, but also the contributions of those who make the system work.

The reality is that despite phenomenal gains there is even more to do. The rapid urbanization of China and its economic success have addressed some issues, but the process has created new ones. For Kunshan the next 10 years will involve a rapid rush to develop a prosperous new urban area which will be home to six to eight million people. Kunshan's preparation for the future follows Shanghai's Expo theme, "Better City, Better Life". What does this mean? It means focusing on developing an attractive living and working environment that can draw and retain high value added industries and people. What is interesting is that although these industries all have export aspects they will position Kunshan for both domestic and international competition. The one certainty is that there will continue to be new problems; for instance, if the Hukou system (China's residency registration system) were to be changed, Kunshan, with its two-to-one migrant population would face a heavy burden that would affect everything from social service systems to reportable GDP.

When I think of Kunshan, the first thing that comes to mind, after the memorable people I have met, is the Goodbaby Company and Mr. Song's story about the duck that is willing to jump into the water first. It underlines one of the things I feel most strongly about China, which is that in many cases it lacks the courage to jump in. Kunshan is an example of what happens when you have the courage to do what needs to be done.

Kunshan is also an example of what people can do, at a time when Chinese officials are often stereotyped as corrupt or self-serving, people forget that unless there was a cadre of people who were willing to support the collective good of society, it would have been impossible for China to have made the phenomenal progress it has made to date. Having over the years met thousands of officials at virtually all levels of government in the US and China, I can attest that the business of the people depends on those who take their responsibilities as a sacred trust, not on systems alone. In Kunshan I met leaders and people who exemplify this truth.

China's success over the last thirty years and Kunshan's over the last twenty years, can not be adequately explained unless you factor in the dedication and efforts of those who created the policies and solutions. These are the parts we do not see, the operational parts where people, policies and action forge the framework of the future. Like the "iceberg" referred to earlier, the people who make Kunshan work are the unseen supporting mass which make its success visible. You may ask why it is necessary to reiterate a point made previously but to understand Kunshan's

Zhouzhuang—future artists at work

future you need to look beyond its economic advantages to the people. In our desire to simplify things we often try to use what we know to algebraically solve for the unknown, but too often we ignore the most important variable, the human aspect, maybe because it is too hard to quantify.

Yes Kunshan's future depends on global and national forces beyond their control; foreign exchange rates, tariffs, commodity prices, comparative labor costs, consumer demand and international relations, but it also depends on the ingenuity of its people to deal with a world that is often harsh and unforgiving. Rather than just riding the crest of the economic wave Kunshan actively plans its economic and social future and most importantly it has the courage and confidence to jump in when it sees an opportunity and say no when it doesn't.

As you digest the comments and outlooks of its leaders, businessmen and people you will see a willingness to learn, plan, take risks and work. But, the difference between Kunshan and cities in the West is the extent and sophistication of its involvement in its economic and social systems. Rather than taking a passive role,

it is an active leader and partner with its industries and companies. It builds its economic strategy the way a nation would, selecting, grouping and nurturing industries which fit its competitive advantages. The difference is that for Kunshan, as well as China, economic development is a tool, an important tool, but none the less a tool in its drive towards social stability. In the West we tend to believe that a prosperous economy will by itself create stable society.

While Kunshan's strategy of combining selective high tech, research facilities and human capital development may not be unique its drive and focus are. Other communities may preach the gospel but with careful planning and hard work Kunshan makes the miracles happen.

If you are a business which is interested in Kunshan, I have included some basic economic and contact data in the Appendix, which you can use to figure out if Kunshan is a place you would like to consider. To give you an idea of the stark differences between Eastern and Western approaches to the role of government in economic development, I have included the following internal projections made by Kunshan about where Kunshan is going. It is important because it demonstrates a number of things: first, the top-down hierarchy of Chinese government, contrast it with the standard political state of the nation report you would get from a Western politician; second, it shows how actively involved local governments are in the economic development of their areas, the closest comparison to it from the West would be a CEO's internal corporate strategy report; third, it demonstrates the consistency of Kunshan's internal and external message, a message which differs in form and substance from the usually undefined goals and promises issued by most government leaders in developed countries. In many ways the report is the best example of the differences between Eastern and Western approaches to government and economic development. It has given me pause for thought about the intrinsic strengths and weaknesses of these different systems and what they

On the right:
Foxconn Group-Apple Computer's main OEM Kunshan Industrial Molding Park

mean for the future.

If you have similar thoughts I suggest you think about visiting Kunshan, especially if you are in Shanghai for the Expo, it will give you a new perspective on what China is and where it is going.

Enjoy and I hope to see you in Kunshan.

Future Development Goals (Kunshan 2009)

Two phases development plan: 2009—2012 and 2013—2015

2009—2012:
- Strengthen our current advanced industries
- Develop four to five complete industrial supply chains to improve our research, manufacturing and sales capabilities in emerging industries such as optical display, IT and network devices, and equipment manufacture
- Emphasize the development of service industries over manufacturing industry
- Increase GDP to RMB 280 billion by 2012 (2009: RMB 175 billion)

Financial service outsourcing center

2013—2015:
- Build three to four new energy/material/technology industries in areas which include solar energy, new energy automobiles and biomedicine
- Be a national level leader in at least two of these industries
- Quicken the pace of economic transition from traditional primary and secondary industries to high value tertiary and service industries.
- Increase GDP to 430 billion yuan by 2015

Future Goals:

2016—2020:
- Pursue new economic initiatives in high value-added niche markets and industries including new energy, new materials and biomedicine
- Increase tertiary industry contributions to GDP to 50% of total local economy
- Increase GDP to 830 billion yuan by 2020

2030:
- Be a research-driven global industrial manufacturing center in a number of diversified new development fields.

Current Plan:

Kunshan has four main industries in which it enjoys an advantage in technology and manufacturing scale which it will support and extend as part of the plan to support future needs:

- Electronic information industry
- Advanced equipment manufacture
- New and high-tech industries
- Modern services

Kunshan has four mainstay industries whose efforts to reach global scale will be supported by direct and indirect means

- Devices manufacture for electronic information industry
- Optoelectrical industry
- Automobile spare parts industry
- Modern logistics industry

Kunshan is pursuing four emerging industries using research and development programs and investment which will be the base of profitable future industry development:

- Modern biotech industry
- New energy and new material industry
- Robot design and manufacture
- Service outsourcing industry

Kunshan has four fundamental industries which will support its efforts to move toward an advanced world-class manufacturing and service center and provide new business and job opportunities:

- Advanced manufacture industry
- Real estate industry
- Trade and commerce industry
- Tourism industry

Kunshan has nine major projects:

1. Increase industrialization by improving the urban infrastructure and amenities
2. Concentrate on strategic industries development
3. Promote research and innovation in science and technology
4. Optimize our industrial zones (in terms of spacing and ecology)
5. Encourage and support the creation and development of locally-owned and manufactured brands
6. Promote entrepreneurship
7. Work closely with and strengthen our Taiwanese industrial supply chains
8. Improve our financial environment and develop a credit guarantee system
9. Pursue human resources clustering

Appendix

City Living Overview

Climate

Kunshan is located in the Yangtze River Delta. It has a subtropical monsoon climate zone, with four distinct seasons, abundant rainfall, and average altitude of 3.4 meters above sea level. The yearly average temperature is 15.5 degrees centigrade, annual average rainfall is 1,097.1 millimeters and annual average sunshine is 2,085.9 hours. Extreme historical temperatures: 39.0°C (2003-08-01) and -11.7°C (1977-01-31).

Housing

Average housing price (about middle level): 6,000-7,000 yuan/m² (approximately $100 per square foot).

Living Environment and Amenities

Schools

There are many universities/colleges in Shanghai, Suzhou and Nanjing. Kunshan has a very strong set of vocational education facilities. Currently, there are more than 20,000 students in seven universities/colleges, including:
- Kunshan TV University;
- Gui Lake Vocational School;
- Application Technology School of Suzhou;
- University, Kunshan Dengyun Science and Technology Vocational Academy;
- Top IT Academy;
- PLA Foreign Languages Institute Kunshan Branch;
- In addition, Kunshan has 32 middle/high schools, three vocational high schools, and a new middle school catering to the children of Taiwanese business people.
- At present, Kunshan is developing a Kunshan College Town, which will comprise Kunshan Dengyun Science and Technology Vocational Academy, Tsinghua Science and Technology Park and Fu Na Film and Video School. US-based Duke University has signed a contract with Kunshan city government to develop a branch in Kunshan in 2011.

Health Care

Kunshan offers better medical care than regular county-level cities in China. In addition to regular hospitals and clinics, there is a non-profit international hospital called Zong Ren Qing Hospital. It was donated and operated by Taiwanese. There are in total 530 beds, as well as both mainland and Taiwan doctors in this hospital.

Moreover, Kunshan is only half an hour away from Shanghai where world-class medical services are available.

Shopping

Two main department stores, which are:

- Kunshan Shopping Mall; and
- Paris Spring Shopping Mall.

General merchandise stores include:

- Wal-Mart;
- Lotus;
- Hualian;
- Auchan Group;
- Da Run Fa, Hymall, E-mart; and
- Jie Qiang.

Convenience stores include:

- 7-Eleven;
- Quik;
- Yangke;
- Kedi; and
- C-Store.

Entertainment

Museums and sports facilities include:

- Kunshan City Public Library;
- Kunshan City Archives Museum;
- Kunqu Opera Museum;
- Kunshan Grand Theater;
- Kunshan Sports Stadium and Arena;
- Kunshan Natatorium; and
- Kunshan Science & Culture Exhibition Center, which provides convention and space for business, culture and art shows.

Resorts and parks:

- Tinglin Park;
- Zhouzhuang, Qiandeng, Jinxi waterside villages;
- Zhaolingshan Liangchu Cultural Heritage (one of 1992 top 10 national archaeological discoveries);
- Tomb of Gu Yanwu;
- Qinfeng Tower;
- Wenchang Pavilion;
- Yangcheng and Dianshan lakes;
- Various water parks, golf courses, yacht clubs and vacation villages; and
- Dan Gui Yuan Theme Park.

Cultural Things-to-do

Kunqu Opera Training Program

Kunshan Small Plum Blossom Performing Group was established in 2009. In addition to Kunqu Opera shows, the group has five Kunqu Opera training centers in Qiandeng, Xinzhen, Bacheng, Yushan and Lujia.

The Kunshan Culture Museum and Children's Palace

These offer art training courses in addition to Kunqu Opera.

Learn Chinese, the traditional painting styles, calligraphy, martial arts, meditation, Buddhism, Taoism, local crafts, cooking, music and visit the hundreds of historical sites in the area.

In August and September, enjoy Oktoberfest in Kunshan, as outdoor tents, entertainment, perfect weather and great beer transform Kunshan into a beer drinker's paradise.

Some suggested things to do in Kunshan

Plan a day trip or stay over night. If you are in Shanghai Kunshan is about a half hour or so away by train depending on where you are. For information about lodging call the Kunshan tourist bureau at 86-512-57592225 or visit them on-line at http://www.kunshan.travel/. In terms of tours, for an additional fee you can join a group tour or hire a local guide from the local tourist bureau.

Visit the waterside town of Zhouzhuang

Zhouzhuang is about 40 minutes from the train station by taxi or bus, the entrance fee is 100 yuan.

Things to do include:
- Walk the ancient stone streets of the town as they wind along the river
- Visit the famous "Double Bridge"
- Watch a Kunqu Opera show at the restored historic theater
- Tour the palatial houses of the Zhang and Shen families
- Take a river taxi tour
- Eat Wansan pork or sample the many tasty local dishes at one of the many restaurants you will encounter.
- Handcraft shopping on Zhenfeng Street
- Boating on Taishidian Lake
- Harvesting your own pearls

Visit the waterside town of Qiandeng

Qiandeng is about 30 minutes from the train station by taxi or bus, the entrance fee is 60 yuan.

Things to do include:
- See the longest stone-paved road in south China
- Sit in the ancient Qinfeng pagoda
- Admire the World's Largest Jade Reclining Buddha at Yanfu Temple
- See a performance of Kunqu Opera in the restored historic stage
- Visit the house of Gu Yanwu one of the pre-eminent philosophers and linguists of his time
- Go to the Datang Ecological Park→Pick organic vegetables and fruits
- Enjoy a glimpse of Kunshan's unchanged rural scenery
- Go to the Cross-straits Flower Fair

Visit the waterside town of Jinxi

Jinxi is about 30 minutes from the train station by taxi or bus, the entrance fee is 50 yuan.

Things to do include:
- See the Chenfei waterside cemetery
- Meditate at the ancient Lotus Pool Temple
- Visit the Wenchang Pavilion
- Go boating on the old river channels of Jinxi
- See the museum of bricks and tiles, understand how artisans created the building blocks of China
- See Eastern China No.1 museum of antiques
- Stop by the Revolutionary Culture Museum and sample Red Tourism

Visit the waterside town of Bacheng

Bacheng is about 30 minutes from the train station by taxi or bus, no entrance fees.

Things to do include:
- Stop at the Week Nine Ecological Farm
- Ride horses
- See the future of Chinese agriculture
- Pick your own vegetables and fruit
- Sample organic food and aquatic products at the ecological restaurant
- Visit the Yangcheng Lake Water Park
- Walk the cobbled stone streets of historic Bacheng
- Visit the Crab Museum and become an expert
- Relax at the Longyunju Teahouse, learn about tea and listen to Pingtan (traditional story telling and ballad singing in the Suzhou dialect)
- Try one of Bacheng's thousand restaurants and if the crabs are in season prepare yourself for a treat.

Tinglin Park

Tinglin Park is about 15 minutes from the train station by taxi or bus, the entrance fee is 20 yuan.

Things to do include:
- Go to the park in the early morning and watch it come alive as the people of Kunshan sing, play, exercise and chat
- See the "Three Treasures" of Kunshan: Kunshan Stone, the Jade Flower, and the Twin-lotus Flower
- Visit the Kunshan History Museum and read about its heroes
- Peruse the Kunqu Opera Museum
- Watch a Kunqu Opera show in the courtyard theater
- Walk the paths of Yufeng Mountain
- Have a sumptuous banquet at the century-old Aozao Noodles Restaurant
- Visit the cross-straits flower exhibition center and see the miniature gardens and potted plants

Tourism Information

Frequently Used Phones

Directory Enquiries	0512-114
Police	0512-110
Fire Emergency	0512-119
Medical Emergency	0512-120
Traffic Emergency	0512-122
Weather Report	0512-96121
Urban Service Center	0512-12345
Customer Complaints	0512-12315
Environmental Complaints	0512-12369
Price Complaints	0512-12358
Labor Complaints	0512-83341202
Tourist Complaints	0512-57531200
Illegal Bus Driver Complaints	0512-83353464
Air Flight Enquiries	0512-57552500
Railway Enquiries	0512-1601066
Bus Enquiries	0512-57312534
Long-distance Bus Enquiries	0512-57386789

Urban Festivals

Name	Date	Place
Kunshan International Culture & Tourism Festival	April to May	Downtown
Kunshan International Beer Festival	Last Thursday in August	Downtown
Kunshan Tinglin Jade Flower Festival	April 15th to May 15th	Tinglin Park
Zhouzhuang Tourism Festival	April	Zhouzhuang Town
Jinxi Tourism Festival	October	Jinxi Town
Qiandeng Tourism Festival	April	Qiandeng Town
Kunshan Bacheng Yangcheng Lake Crabs Festival	Late September	Bacheng Town

Main Hotels

Name	Level	Address	Telephone
Swissotel Kunshan	5 stars	No. 387 Mid Qianjin Road	0512-57885788
Kunshan Huaqiao Hilton Double Tree	5 stars	No.2 Zhaofeng Road, Huaqiao Zone	0512-57602222
Kunshan Fairmont Yangcheng Lake Hotel	5 stars	No.3668 Maanshan West Road, Zhengyi Town	0512 5780 0888
Kunshan Hotel	4 stars	No.99 Renmin North Road	0512-57888000
Kunshan Venice Holiday Hotel	4 stars	No.18 Minquan Road, Bacheng Town	0512-57016353
Zhouzhuang Hotel	3 stars	No.88 Daqiao North Road, Zhouzhuang Town	0512-57213018
Hanting Chain Hotel	Budget Hotel	No.35 Renmin South Road	0512-57886188
Long River Garden	Budget Hotel	Crossing of Changjiang North Road and Xinpu Road	0512-57869888

Investment Contact Information

Website of Kunshan Municipal People's Government
http://www.ks.gov.cn

Kunshan News
http://www.ksnews.cn

Foreign Trade & Economic Cooperation Bureau of Kunshan
(Kunshan Foreign Investment Promotion Service Center)
TEL: 0512-57312188
FAX: 0512-57311560
Email: wjmj@ks.gov.cn

Investment Promotion Bureau of KETD
TEL: 0512-57329271
FAX: 0512-57329291
Email:zs@ketd.gov.cn

Investment Promotion Bureau of Huaqiao Economic Development Zone
TEL: 0512-57696596
FAX: 0512-57608618
Email:stevenwu01@sohu.com

Investment Promotion Bureau of KSND
TEL: 0512-57790069
FAX: 0512-57790180
Email:info@ksnd.gov.cn

Kunshan Administrative Service Center
TEL: 0512-57379095
FAX: 0512-57379096
Email:xzfw@ks.gov.cn

Kunshan Euro-American Investment Promotion Center
TEL: 0512-57505006
FAX: 0512-57501865
Email:wjm_lh@ks.gov.cn

General Office of Kunshan Association of Foreign-funded Enterprises
TEL: 0512-57559251
FAX: 0512-57501862
Email:wjm_xhb@ks.gov.cn

Kunshan Taiwan Businessmen's Association
TEL: 0512-57333628
FAX: 0512-57333630
Email:ks57333628@163.com

Kunshan Municipal People's Government Beijing Office
TEL: 010-64410386
FAX: 010-65537073

Kunshan Municipal People's Government Shenzhen Office
TEL: 0755-83020166
FAX: 0755-83020199

Kunshan Municipal People's Government Tokyo Office, Japan
TEL: 0081-3-53313850
FAX: 0081-3-53313844

Kunshan Land and Resources Information (zoning, land use policies, land purchase and lease requirements, construction costs, and approval process) Contact: http://www.landks.com

Kunshan Bureau of Housing and Urban-Rural Development (Infrastructure information) Contact: http://www.kscein.gov.cn

Index

图书在版编目(CIP)数据

昆山轨迹：英文/（美）唐根
著.—北京：外文出版社, 2010
（中国城记）
ISBN 978-7-119-06432-1

Ⅰ.①昆… Ⅱ.①唐… Ⅲ.①昆
山市－概况－英文
Ⅳ.①K925.34

中国版本图书馆CIP数据核字
(2010)第076232号

总策划：黄友义　张国华

统筹：徐发波　管爱国

创意：杭颖　周鸣

项目指导：
徐明强　呼宝民　李振国
邵东　解琛　胡开敏

英文审定：李振国

责任编辑：文芳　欧阳伟萍

总序翻译：欧阳伟萍

英文审校：梁良兴

图片提供：
昆山市委宣传部
昆山市住房和城乡建设局

编务：
阳世坤　李金海
戴小华　高丽丽

总设计：
刘扬设计工作室，柏林

排版制作：邓翔

印刷监制：张国祥

昆山轨迹

[美]艾那·唐根(Einar Tangen)著

©2010 外文出版社

出版发行：
外文出版社

地址：
中国北京百万庄大街24号

邮政编码: 100037

网址：http://www.flp.com.cn

电话：
008610-68320579 （总编室）
008610-68995852 （发行部）
008610-68327750 （版权部）

制版：
北京红色调文化艺术有限公司

印刷：
北京雷杰印刷有限公司

开本：
787mm×1092mm 1/16

印张：12.5

2010年第1版第1次印刷

（英）

ISBN 978-7-119-06432-1

10800 (平装)

The Kunshan Way

First Edition 2010

Executive Directors:
Huang Youyi, Zhang Guohua

Project Coordinators:
Xu Fabo, Guan Aiguo

Concept Developer:
Hang Ying, Zhou Ming

Consultants:
Xu Mingqiang, Hu Baomin,
Li Zhenguo, Shao Dong,
Xie Chen, Hu Kaimin

Senior Editor:
Li Zhenguo

Editors:
Wen Fang, Ouyang Weiping

Proofreader:
Liang Liangxing

Photographers:
Publicity Department of
Kunshan Municipal Committee
of the CPC, Kunshan Bureau
of Housing and Urban-Rural
Development

Contributors:
Yang Shikun, Li Jinhai,
Dai Xiaohua, Gao Lili

Designer:
Yang Liu Design

Digital Compositor:
Deng Xiang

ISBN 978-7-119-06432-1

© Foreign Languages Press,
Beijing, China, 2010

Published by Foreign
Languages Press
24 Baiwanzhuang Road, Beijing
100037, China
http://www.flp.com.cn

Distributed by China International Book Trading Corporation

35 Chegongzhuang Xilu, Beijing
100044, China
P.O. Box 399, Beijing, China

*Printed in the People's Republic
of China*